ORIENTEERING

Steven Boga

STACKPOLE BOOKS

Copyright © 1997 by Stackpole Books

Published by
STACKPOLE BOOKS
5067 Ritter Road
Mechanicsburg, PA 17055
www.stackpolebooks.com

Printed in the United States of America

10   9   8   7

First edition

Cover design by Wendy A. Reynolds

Photographs by William J. Boga

Photograph on page 9 courtesy of Don Geary

Library of Congress Cataloging-in-Publication Data

Boga, Steve, 1947–
        Orienteering / by Steve Boga; [photographs by William J. Boga].—1st ed.
                p.   cm.
        ISBN 0-8117-2870-6 (alk. paper)
        1. Orienteering. I. Title
    GV200.4.B64   1997
    796.5'1—dc20   96-24380
                                                                              CIP

ISBN 978-0-8117-2870-6

CONTENTS

INTRODUCTION

The babble of a brook, the sensual caress of a breeze against the skin—these shape us in ways we do not fully understand. I have a dual suggestion that will cater to kids and adults alike: create more orienteering courses and add orienteering to school curricula. Why orienteering? Because of the unique mix of fun, fitness, mental challenge, and immersion in natural beauty that orienteering offers. At top levels, participants compete against both themselves and the terrain, relying on speed, endurance, decision-making, and navigational skills to find their way through the woods to control sites. As physical skills diminish with age, orienteers can compensate with experience, which helps to make "O" a lifetime sport. It is an outdoor adventure, but one that offers a wide range of skill and exertion levels. Thus it has allure for the trained athlete, the ardent environmentalist, and the family that just wants a purposeful walk in the woods.

Although orienteering is more of a technique sport than a rules sport, you will enjoy your first outing more and probably stay with the sport longer if you understand the basics. Here's what to expect:

- Orienteering events are usually held in areas that are both wooded and open, and feature some obvious landmarks, such as fences, trails, knolls, and reentrants.
- Your goal in orienteering is to find the fastest, albeit safe, route between a series of marked features in the terrain, using a compass and a detailed map. Route selection is at the heart of the sport, and a big reason for its unique appeal.
- A competition course should be unfamiliar to you.
- Several courses are offered at a meet. Which course you choose depends on age, fitness level, and experience. Beginners, intermediates, and advanced orienteers visit

different control features on different length courses. Shorter, technically difficult courses exist for older, advanced competitors.

- Orienteers don't start all at once, but at regular intervals to preclude one competitor shadowing another. The start is usually located within a few minutes' walk from the registration table, along a path marked by colored streamers.

- Besides a map and compass, you will carry a description sheet, detailing the location of each control to be visited. Each control is identified on the description sheet by a code, either two letters (AG, BF) or two or three digits (24, 132). The code also appears on the control flag attached to each control feature. Matching control codes is your check that you have found the right control.

- On intermediate and advanced courses, International Orienteering Federation (IOF) symbols are used. See figure 8 for a sample description sheet and a decoding.

- You are issued a control card that lists your name and course level.

- If the control features are not already circled on the map, you must copy your course from a master map near the start. For intermediates and above, time spent copying the course onto your map usually counts toward total time.

- Knowing where you are at all times is the key to successful orienteering, and good map-reading skills are essential.

- At each control, you check that the code on the control flag matches the code on the description sheet, then use the punch available at each site to mark your control card, proof that you visited that control. Controls must be punched in the correct order. For example, you may not punch 5 until after 4 has been found.

- After completing the series of controls, you will follow a streamered route to the finish.

- As you cross the finish line, your finish time is recorded, and meet officials calculate the total elapsed time for the course. The control card is checked to make sure all controls were visited and that the right boxes were punched. The final results are posted in the finish area.

- You exchange glad tidings with the other participants, feeling gratified and eager to try again.

Besides the usual acknowledgements, such as my parents, and my wife Karen and my editor David Uhler for putting up with me, I'd like to offer special thanks to the United States Orienteering Federation, most notably executive director Robin Shannonhouse and director of marketing Jon Nash.

My deepest gratitude is reserved for Joe and James Scarborough, who submitted to more than the usual number of interviews, and especially to Joe for his editorial input.

History of Orienteering

Orienteering, the art of cross-country navigation with map and compass, began in late nineteenth century Scandinavia as a military exercise. Credit Maj. Ernst Killander, a Swedish scout leader, for popularizing it as a sport. Noting that fewer and fewer Swedish youths were participating in track and field, he decided to use the natural Swedish countryside to motivate young runners. Hoping to make running more appealing, he set courses in the forest and issued maps and compasses to the competitors. Those first races were a great success, and he was sufficiently encouraged to try to extend orienteering to the masses.

Killander held the first major orienteering contest in March 1919, with 155 participants on a course fifteen kilometers south of Stockholm. A monument marks the site as the birthplace of orienteering.

Killander continued to spread his gospel, and in 1922 the first district championship was held. In those days, the courses required more aerobic fitness than navigational prowess, because the checkpoints runners had to find were set up on large, obvious features of the landscape. This was mainly a concession to the inadequacy of Swedish maps, which tended to be more decorative than cartographic.

By the mid-1930s, map quality had greatly improved, and so map-reading skills became more important. Now the prize went to the complete orienteer, not just the fittest athlete.

The sport continued to spread throughout Sweden, and in 1936 a national organization was formed. The Swedish Orienteering Federation (Svenska Orienteringforbundet, or SOFT), run by former members of the Swedish Boy Scouts, soon controlled all foot orienteering events, including the first national championships in 1937. Orienteering by skis, another popular activity, was directed by the national ski association.

Acknowledging that orienteering promoted both good health and a working knowledge of geography, the Swedish government made it a compulsory subject in Swedish schools. Even today, the study of maps is part of the curriculum for Swedish nine-year-olds. At age fourteen, Swedish children compete for a special orienteering proficiency badge. They must pass a test not only on navigation but on conservation and nature lore.

Orienteering quickly spread through Scandinavia and beyond. Orienteering is a national pastime in Norway and Finland, and there are annual Nordic championships. In 1963, 182,000 people participated in a promotional event in Sweden.

Today, the granddaddy event of the year is the O-Ringen, a five-day orienteering festival held in Sweden. As many as 25,000 orienteers gather from all over the world every summer to compete on 100 courses.

The International Orienteering Federation (IOF) was established at a meeting in Copenhagen in 1961. Within three years, eleven countries were affiliated with the IOF: Bulgaria, Denmark, Czechoslovakia, East and West Germany, Finland, Norway, Hungary, Austria, Switzerland, and Sweden.

In 1962 Norway hosted the first European Championship, a biennial event that endures today. That same year, Baron "Rak" Lagerfelt of the Stockholm Orienteering Club traveled to Scotland in an attempt to spread the "O" word. Scotland, with some of its terrain similar to Sweden's, was receptive to Lagerfelt. The Scots, outdoorsy types by nature, immediately saw potential in orienteering and offered Lagerfelt the support of the Scottish Council of Physical Recreation. The result of that alliance was a comprehensive training program and an annual national championship.

Orienteering soon reached south to England, where it was embraced by an enthusiastic fringe of a populace already accustomed to taking bracing walks. In 1964 England's first orienteering club was formed, and in January 1965 a group of teachers in Surrey County came out in favor of orienteering classes. A flurry of world-class runners, including Gordon Pirie, Chris Brasher, John Disley, and Roger Bannister (first person to break the four-minute mile), decided to take a shot at this new sport.

The winner of the first race was a schoolboy fresh from geography class at his Walton-on-Thames school. Former 5,000-meter record holder Gordon Pirie raced back and forth through Hurt Woods for two hours, finding by sheer chance one of the six controls scattered over a few square miles of forest and sandstone ridge. He eventually had to ask an old lady for directions back to the starting point.

A competitor by nature, Pirie went off to do his homework. A month later, the schoolboy was struggling to finish in the top ten, while Pirie, adroit by now with his compass, finished second in a field of sixty.

According to English orienteer John Disley, this pattern can be expected every time orienteering is introduced into a community. "First, the tortoises win comfortably with the hares leaping all over the countryside from hill to hill, finding the red and white banners only by chance. Then the hares go away and do some studying and begin to run most of the time in the right direction, and to record better times than the tortoises. Finally, deprived of the taste of honey that early success has given them, the tortoises shrug off their shells and start to go out running-training. Hence the cycle is complete and now the orienteering community allows success to go to those who are both clever and fast, skillful with map and compass, and fit in the lungs and legs."

North America

The first orienteering event in North America was on November 20, 1941, at Dartmouth College, in Hanover, New Hampshire, organized by Piltti Heiskanen, a Finnish army officer. But the sport went moribund when Heiskanen left town in April 1943.

In 1946 Bjorn Kjellstrom, the co-inventor of the protractor-type, liquid-filled compass, moved from Sweden to the United States, where he began to support and sponsor orienteering events. Throughout the forties and fifties, he introduced orienteering to people all over North America.

Kjellstrom's efforts spurred a greater understanding of compass and map, but the sport of orienteering gained popularity at a snail's pace until the late sixties, when Harald Wibye of Norway appeared. Wibye helped set up clubs and activities all over the continent, beginning with a competition on November 5, 1967, at Valley Forge, Pennsylvania. The new group that sponsored the event, now called the Delaware Valley Orienteering Association, is today the largest orienteering club in the United States.

During Wibye's two-year stay in North America, he also founded Canada's first real orienteering club and produced the continent's first modern color-coded orienteering maps, an essential ingredient in the sport today. Wibye also helped organize "O" activities for the military. The U.S. Marine Corps Physical Fitness Academy at Quantico, Virginia, held its first public orienteering competition in 1968, an event largely orchestrated by Wibye.

Bob Shoptaw, the second assistant director at Quantico, was the primary founder of the U.S. Orienteering Federation (USOF), established in 1971. Shoptaw worked to introduce orienteering to the entire Marine Corps. The goal, according to a former Quantico orienteer, was "to build the most effective land-navigation training strategy of any branch of the service."

The overlapping presence on the continent of Kjellstrom and Wibye, as well as the dedicated labor of other visionaries, accounted for North American orienteering's first true growth spurt. Eight years after it was founded, the USOF had nineteen hundred members in eighty clubs.

At the same time, a strong military-orienteering connection continued: the first six U.S. men's orienteering titles were won by Marines, a streak that was eventually broken by Peter Gagarin of

Massachusetts. Gagarin would go on to be U.S. champion five times. He also founded and coached the U.S. team, which has competed in each of the biennial World Orienteering Championships since 1974. Gagarin's success as a master orienteer in the eighties and nineties ranks him at the top of the all-time non-European competitors. Gagarin, now in his fifties, is still one of the country's top orienteers, although his dominance was passed on to Eric Weyman and later Mikell Platt.

Membership in orienteering clubs rose during the eighties, although the number of USOF clubs declined. A few clubs were doing the lion's share of the work. The New England club grew to 700 members; the Hudson Valley Orienteers began hosting national and international events; the Delaware Valley Orienteering Association coordinated the 1982 and 1992 U.S. Championships. A whopping 705 orienteers competed in the 1982 event.

Even larger U.S. events were the 1990 Asia-Pacific Orienteering Carnival in Washington State, with 869 contestants, mostly from other countries; several of Dave Linthicum's annual Boy Scout orienteering championships near Baltimore, one of which attracted 1,095 orienteers; and the 1993 World Championships in New York State.

Despite a steady growth in overall U.S. orienteering numbers, youth participation hit an all-time low in the nineties, placing the United States dead last in that category. In terms of both popularity and excellence, the United States continues to lag far behind the world-class orienteering nations. Some say the sport has a misleading image as a casual activity that lacks the spark of tough competition. Dave Linthicum, USOF librarian, suggests that North America is unique in the orienteering world in the way that compass games are often erroneously called "orienteering." The USOF is striving to counter this misperception, focusing on the European method of teaching beginners how to read maps.

Orienteering optimists see the glass as half full. Participation in the sport is on the rise, they point out. In 1990, 41,508 people entered 635 events, and membership in USOF and member clubs had climbed to 6,650.

Getting Started

Our minds are lazier than our bodies.
—La Rochefoucauld

YOUR FIRST COURSE

Orienteering welcomes beginners. All you really need to attend your first O-meet are some old clothes and the energy to try something new.

Most meets offer four to six courses of varying difficulties, each identified by color. From easy to hardest, they are White, Yellow, Orange, Brown, Green, Red, and Blue. Most events have miniclinics for beginners, and many include a String course for young children. Adult beginners should always start on the White course, which is designed to acquaint you with the rules and basic techniques of the sport.

When you register, you will be assigned a starting time—contestants start at different times to make sure they work independently—and you will receive three items. The most important is a specially drawn map with many symbols in different colors. This map will be topographic (showing the land's contour) and it will give very fine detail, such as "small gully" or "large boulder." The scale for distances will be metric, using centimeters instead of inches.

You will use this map to navigate to checkpoints that are flagged in the field with orange-and-white nylon boxes. Those checkpoints, called *controls,* are shown on orienteering maps by small circles. However, those controls may not appear on your map yet. If they don't, you must copy them from a master map.

To help you find the controls, you will receive a control description sheet, along with a control card that you will punch to prove you were there (figs 1 and 2).

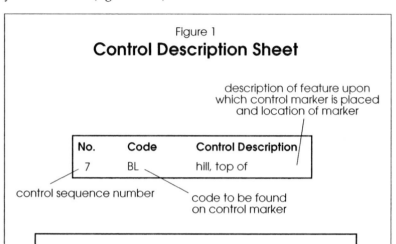

Figure 1
Control Description Sheet

description of feature upon which control marker is placed and location of marker

No.	Code	Control Description
7	BL	hill, top of

control sequence number

code to be found on control marker

YELLOW (4.0 km, Max climb 150 m)

No.	Code	Control Description
1	GK	semi-open area, N. E. corner, inside
2	BG	trail bend
3	EU	hill, top of
4	EY	trail bend
5	EN	ruin, N. side
6	EG	trail and fence crossing
7	BL	trail junction
8	EV	hill, top of
9	BA	trail junction
10	ET	trail bend
11	EL	semi-open area, S. W. corner, inside
12	FX	semi-open area, N. W. corner, inside

Follow marked route to FINISH—200 meters

Safety bearing: 90° east

Figure 2

A Completed Control Card

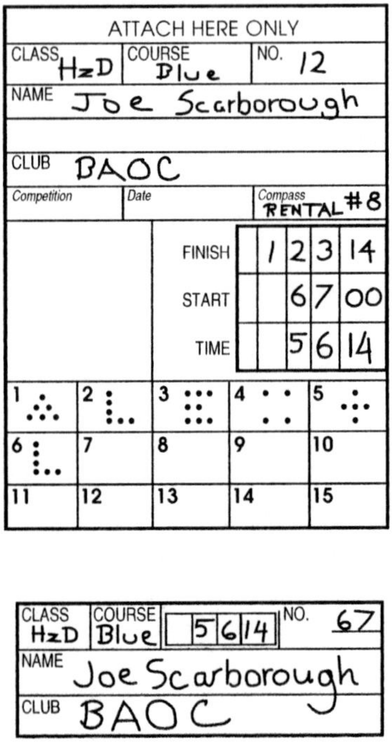

ATTACH HERE ONLY			
CLASS HzD	COURSE Blue	NO. 12	
NAME Joe Scarborough			

CLUB BAOC			
Competition	Date	Compass RENTAL #8	

	FINISH	1	2	3	14
	START		6	7	00
	TIME		5	6	14

1	2	3	4	5
6	7	8	9	10
11	12	13	14	15

CLASS HzD	COURSE Blue	5 6 14	NO. 67
NAME Joe Scarborough			
CLUB BAOC			

The first control might read:

1 (AB) Stream Bend, So. Side

This tells you that the marker for control No. 1 will have the code (AB) and will be hanging at the south side of the stream bend shown on your map at the center of the first circle. A needle punch will be hanging from each marker; use it to punch the appropriate box on your control card. Each punch is distinctive and confirms your visit to that control.

Novice courses are designed to give everyone a good, safe, encouraging time. The first few controls are especially easy to find, instilling in the beginner some much-needed self-confidence. And, as orienteer, author, and ex-Olympian John Disley says: "The intense satisfaction of finding a marker exactly where you expected it to be is a delight that has to be experienced to be believed."

Maybe you can imagine it: You climb a series of switchbacks toward the crest of a ridge. It's tough going, but you persevere. Breathing steadily, you reach the top and look down upon the very valley you expected to see. As you descend, you hear the gurgle of water and know it is the creek marked on the map. You find the footbridge just upstream from the confluence of two streams—and on it an orange-and-white control marker. It is your first marker! You are flooded with joy.

When you have successfully navigated the course and punched in the correct boxes on your control card, you head for the finish. There, your finish time is recorded and your card is examined. Your name and time are posted by course or age group, and after all the participants are off the course, you are given a final position. The winner is the one who visits all the controls in the correct order in the shortest elapsed time.

In most cases, first-timers go home happy, satisfied, and aware of how lightly they have penetrated this new world. In many cases, they are sufficiently challenged by the experience to return and try again.

HOW TO PREPARE
Things to Bring
Bring a compass with a rotating baseplate (Silva type) if you have one, although it is not essential on a beginner's course. Often, the host club will have them available for rent. Later, you can purchase one from a camping store or from an orienteering vendor. Make sure it has a clear plastic baseplate designed for orienteering. A lanyard, or cord, can help you keep track of your compass.

Wear comfortable walking clothes that can take a little dirt.

An orienteering compass has a clear plastic baseplate.

In cold weather, wear several thin layers and a daypack. As you exercise and warm up, you can remove layers and stash them in your daypack. In warm weather, wear light, loose pants. Shorts are comfortable—until you go off-trail and start wading through brush or heavy forest. Bring drinking water and something to eat afterward.

Registration

When you arrive at an orienteering event, check in first at the registration table. Registration is usually open for a specified time. You can arrive and sign in any time during that period, although the beginner's clinic is usually early.

Sometimes you get a good walk in even before the meet starts.

Check in at the registration table when you arrive.

After you pay a small fee and sign a waiver, you will receive the map, control card, and control description sheet. A map case (a clear plastic bag) is usually available to help keep your map, card, and description sheet organized and dry.

Fill out your control card completely, noting the course you will do. Don't be afraid to ask for help or advice. The control description sheet will make more sense once you have copied the course onto your map.

Your first time out, you will be testing your mettle against the White course. Sign up to go out alone or in a small group of two or three. Children will benefit most if at least one adult goes out with them. Try to have a map for each person over age eight or nine.

When you're finished with the preliminaries, get a starting time from the starter.

You will receive a starting time from the starter.

Beginner's Clinic

At most meets, someone will give periodic briefings for beginners. This short lecture will give first-timers the tips they need to finish the White course. This is a good time to ask questions.

One question you might want to ask is how to learn more about the sport. Someone from the host club should be able to tell you, at the very least, which books to read and when future events and clinics are scheduled.

Here's how Joe Scarborough, who has given dozens of beginner clinics, goes about it:

Good morning. I'm Joe Scarborough and welcome to orienteering. I'm not going to talk much about the compass but about map reading, the essence of the sport, and about its basic procedures and rules. By procedures, I mean what you have to do to get around the course.

Presumably, you are new to orienteering and have registered for the White course. You have a map, a control card, and a description sheet. The White course is designed as an introduction to the sport, as well as competition for boys and girls twelve and under. The controls are usually on obvious line features, like streams or trails, and you can usually do the course in less than an hour.

If you have not done so already, you will get a starting time from the starter. You will start at four-minute intervals, individually or in groups, one control card each. When the starter blows the whistle, you will head for control No. 1, where you will find an orange-and-white flag. The flag will have a two-letter, or a two- or three-number, code that corresponds to the code on your description sheet. There will be a punch by the flag. Use it to punch box No. 1 on your control card.

Then you proceed around the course, visiting the controls in order until you reach the finish, usually not far from the start.

Now, how do you get to the first control? I have simplified the process of land navigation—orienteering—to eight steps. Whether you're a beginner or an elite orienteer, you will basically do all eight of these all of the time, though not always in this order. The more advanced you become, the more subconscious and automatic the steps become.

Step No. 1: Find north. This is easy—the red end of your needle should always point north. Advanced orienteers don't necessarily use the compass to find north. You can also do this by turning the map so that it lines up with the terrain, which is step No. 2.

Step No. 2: Orient the map. Place your compass on your map and rotate your body until the magnetic north lines on the map line up with the north-pointing needle. Keep the map oriented through the following steps.

Step No. 3: Find your location on the map. If you're standing at the start, you've got it made—you're at the start triangle.

Step No. 4: Pick out features around you. First on the map, then on the ground, look for prominent features. Whether it's a stream on your right, a cliff on your left, relate the ground features to the corresponding symbols on the map.

Step No. 5: Face the direction of travel. Keeping the map oriented, move your body around the map until you are facing the next control or an intermediate objective. You have already done a lot, and you haven't even left the starting line.

Step No. 6: Choose your route. You are facing the first control, but unless you are following a straight trail, you will have to adjust your direction of travel. On the White course, you will usually follow an obvious line feature, like a trail. On Yellow and above, finding the optimum route usually means shortcutting.

Step No. 7: Pick out a prominent feature ahead. First on the map, then on the ground, look for a prominent landmark. Look as far ahead as possible. Say you want to reach a trail junction that is just beyond a sharp bend. You can't see the junction, but you can see the bend, and so you know which way to move and about how far it is.

Step No. 8: Proceed to that feature. Follow your chosen route. As you change direction, remember to rotate the map to keep it oriented. Move your thumb along the map to track your progress.

Repeat those steps, moving from control to control. You can do the White course without pace counting or taking bearings. It's more a matter of relating the features on the map to the features on the ground. That's the main skill of orienteering, at any level. If you can do that and keep moving at a fast pace, that's effective orienteering.

Finally, remember to have fun out there. You're learning, so don't worry too much if some things don't come naturally. There are a lot of people around to help. If you ask questions, and come back and try again, it will gradually come to you.

Warm-up

Whether you're a beginner or a veteran, you should warm up prior to the start. The length and intensity of the warm-up will vary, but the basic components are similar:

- Walk and jog to increase the body temperature and the temperature of the working muscles;
- Stretch to increase the range of motion of the muscles and joints;
- Increase the intensity of the walk-jog, perhaps to a run.

The following chart offers an example of a warm-up routine for beginning, intermediate, and advanced orienteers:

Beginner	Intermediate	Advanced
Walk 3–5 minutes	Walk/jog 5–7 minutes	Walk/jog 10 minutes
Stretch 5 minutes	Stretch 5–10 minutes	Stretch 10–15 minutes
Brisk walk/jog 3 minutes	Jog or run 5 minutes	Run 10 minutes

Warm up with a brisk walk or a slow jog.

How to Start, Go, and Finish

Master Maps. Either before or after your start time, depending on the rules, you may have to copy the course onto your map. Even if you are copying it after you have officially started, copy it carefully, because a mistake here can cost you dearly later. The start area is marked with a triangle; each control is marked with a 6-millimeter circle and a sequence number; the finish is depicted by a double circle.

You have to be focused when you copy the route from the master map.

Using a red pen, draw a circle where each control flag is supposed to be (it should be in the center of the circle). If the location is unclear, consult the control description. Number the circles in the correct order and link them with a line (fig 3). Be careful that the circles don't obscure important information on the map.

Planning a Route. To plan your route to the first control, find your place on the map shown by the start triangle. Relate the features nearby to those depicted on the map. Turn the map so that it matches the terrain. Now determine which way to go to the first control. On the White course, there will always be one or more line

Figure 3
Planning a Route

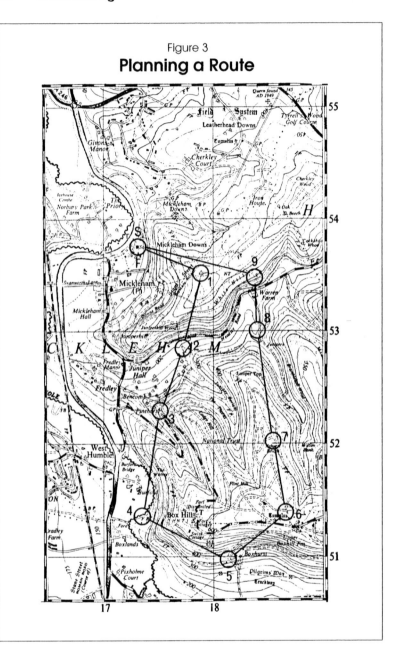

features upon which to rely. Identify the type of feature you are looking for. If you are in a group, do it aloud to involve your children or partners. Don't expect too much of beginners, lest they get frustrated; on the other hand, let them participate in the decision-making or they will get bored. Most of all, don't lose sight of the overriding goal—to have fun roaming through nature.

At the finish, peruse the results board that is posted. It may be enlightening—and humbling—to compare your results with others who did the same course.

Moving Up

After beginners have a handle on simple linear navigation, they may be ready for the Yellow course. At that level, they will have to make multiple decisions on each leg. Instructors can tag along with beginners, letting them navigate but preventing big mistakes. Later, beginners can do the course alone.

The Yellow course tends to follow trails and other linear features, but usually its controls are features just off the trail. Yellow orienteers must do more than simply choose which trail to follow. This new strategy often involves an attack point, a feature such as a river bend, hilltop, or trail junction that tells you when to head off the trail to find the control.

Route choice now becomes more important. You need to ask yourself questions: "What's the surest route? Is there a catching feature—lake, cliff, trail—that will tell me I've gone too far?"

Etiquette and Safety

Rather than focusing on competition, beginners should concentrate on learning and having fun. For your own safety and the safety and well-being of others, pay attention to the following points of etiquette:

- Read all information before starting, especially safety warnings.
- Be quiet in the master map area.
- Do not tail other competitors.
- Do not linger at the controls, lest you give away the location to others.

- Observe out-of-bounds restrictions.
- Report in at the finish within three hours, even if you don't complete the course. This is critical to avoid a massive manhunt.

Physical and Psychological Fitness

Orienteering is a physical sport that places unique demands on the body. Running and fast walking are an important part of any training program, but competitive orienteers must also work on balance, agility, and footwork by practicing movement over rough terrain. Advanced training should eventually include rapid movement through various vegetation and terrain, and lots of hill running.

Beginners and youngsters, however, should focus on regular exercise rather than on intense training. Hiking, biking, skiing, soccer, orienteering, and normal play will all improve aerobic fitness.

If you want newcomers to stick with orienteering, try not to rush them. Let them progress slowly, mastering the skills necessary

Prepare for competition by practicing movement over rough terrain.

to succeed at a more basic course before moving on to a more difficult one. This will foster self-confidence. Emphasize mastery of
skills over competitive victories. Help them see the big picture,
focusing on orienteering as a lifetime sport. Pushing novices too far
too fast can promote frustration, causing them to quit.

As orienteers improve, however, they may crave competition.
Beware of rising expectations that can easily exceed results. The
road to excellence is not a smooth, even, upward slope but rather a
series of relatively brief spurts of progress, each of which is followed by a slight decline to a plateau somewhat higher than the
previous one. You had better learn to enjoy the plateaus, because
that's where you'll spend most of your time.

Young orienteers should have breaks from the pressure of competition. Encourage their participation in "fun" events that play
down the competitive aspect of orienteering. Remind them that
cementing skills and having fun should be the primary goals.

SPECIAL TERMS

It is helpful to have some familiarity with the basic lexicon of
the sport. Here are the most important terms (others are in the
Glossary):

Attack Point. A distinct point, possibly on a *handrail* close to the
control. It should be easy to find, allowing you to run as fast as you
can to get there.

Bearing. The direction of travel from your present location to
another location, as determined by a compass.

Catching Feature. A large or elongated feature that is difficult to
miss. You use a catching feature—a lake, for example, or a road—to
"catch" you if you miss the control.

Compass. While a compass is advised for the White course, it is
required for Yellow and above. The most common orienteering
compass is the rotating baseplate (Silva) type, in which the compass
needle sits in the center of a liquid-damped housing set on a clear
plastic baseplate. With this type of compass, you can determine, set,
and follow a bearing, the angle of the line you intend to follow. This
is especially helpful in the absence of any obvious features.

Contour Interval. The vertical distance between contour lines. The contour interval for many topos (topographic maps) is 20 feet. That means if you walk from one line to the next, you are climbing or dropping 20 feet. Orienteering maps are entirely metric, with a typical contour interval of five meters.

Contour Line. A brown line connecting points of equal elevation on topographic maps. Any point on a single contour line is the same elevation as any other point on that line. Walk along a single contour line and you will not go up or down hill. Contour lines may touch but never cross. You gain or lose elevation when you travel from one line to another. Lines close to one another indicate steep terrain, and lines farther apart show the opposite.

Controls. The mapped features toward which you are navigating, the checkpoints on an orienteering course. Identified in the field by orange-and-white nylon markers that look like box kites, they are shown at the center of circles on your map.

Course. The series of controls shown on the map as circles connected by straight lines.

Handrail. Line features, such as streams or trails, that run parallel to one's direction of travel, thereby aiding navigation. Handrails are features that you can "hang on" to.

Leg. The part of the course between two consecutive controls.

Linear Feature. A trail, stream, fence, wall, or other feature that is basically linear, in contrast to point features (boulders) and area features (clearings).

Map. All maps have three things in common: They are representations of some place, they use symbols, and they use some kind of scale. City and state maps show the terrain as though it were all one level (planimetric maps); topographic maps use contour lines to show the shape of the land, or topography.

Orienteering maps are topos made to a common set of standards used all over the world. Standard orienteering maps are printed in five colors, with each color representing a different type of feature:

Black: Man-made features, such as buildings, roads, bridges, trails, train tracks, power lines, cemeteries, and fences; rock features, such as cliffs and boulders.

Blue: Water features, such as lakes, ponds, rivers, intermittent streams, uncrossable marshes, crossable seasonal marshes, and springs.

Brown: Topographic features, such as hills, valleys, ridges, ditches, and depressions. Interpreting these features is not required of beginners.

Green: Restricted runnability and visibility. Dark green, often referred to as "fight," should be avoided. The lightest green is passable, but at a slower speed than for white or yellow.

Yellow: Clearings and fields.

White: Forested and runnable.

The shadings and patterns of the various colors are fairly intuitive. For example, light green suggests light brush, and dark green denser brush. Trails shown with thick dashed lines are wider than trails with thin lines.

Reentrant. A small valley.

Scale. The relative size of a map to the area it represents. Scale is usually expressed as a ratio, such as 1:10,000, where 1 millimeter on the map represents 10 meters on the ground. The term also refers to the map symbol, usually resembling a ruler, that graphically shows you how many inches (or centimeters) represent a mile (or kilometer) on that particular map.

Spur. A small ridge or protrusion on a hillside.

ORIENTEERING FOR CHILDREN
Getting Used to Nature
Young orienteers need to become comfortable moving through terrain. Hiking and camping are good preparatory activities to build self-confidence and a sense of security, permitting them to concentrate on new orienteering skills as they are introduced.

String Course
For children as young as toddlers, there is often a special orienteering course called a String course. It is even easier than the White course, the usual starting point for beginners. The entire route is marked by a continuous length of ribbon, twine, or tape, so that no one gets lost. Figure 4 is a map of a typical String course. When

children reach each circled spot on the map, they find an orange-and-white nylon marker. Eventually, the string leads them back to the finish, usually the same area as the start.

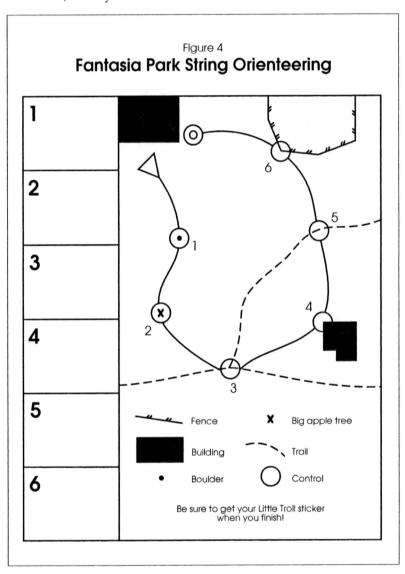

Figure 4
Fantasia Park String Orienteering

String courses are a great jumping-off point for young, beginning orienteers. They offer fun, exercise, and an introductory exposure to maps. As children become more adept at finding their way in the woods, their self-confidence grows and their capabilities expand.

Organizing a String-O Event. If you wish to create a String course, you will need the following materials:

- String, which can be surveyor's tape, twine, colored string, ribbon, or almost anything else that is visible, durable, and easy to roll out. Surveyor's tape, a colored one-inch-wide band of nonadhesive plastic tape, works particularly well. Stretchable, waterproof, highly visible, and inexpensive, it is available in 50-meter rolls from hardware stores and orienteering vendors. If ripped, it can be easily retied.

- Spool, for rolling the string in and out. You can use a spool designed for extension cords, available at hardware stores, or make a simple spool from a cardboard tube (fig 5). A plastic lid will help keep yarn from sliding off the tube. To roll out the string, put a stick through the center and walk backward—carefully.

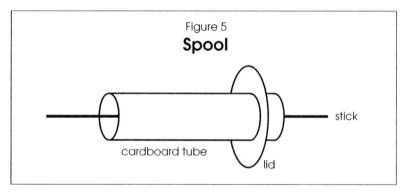

Figure 5
Spool

stick

cardboard tube

lid

- Map (see below for making the map).
- Control markers—usually five to eight orange-and-white nylon markers, just like the ones grown-ups use, or, alternatively, miniature paper versions.

- Stickers, punches, or hand stamps (nontoxic ink), placed at each control. If a different design is used for each control, it serves as a code to confirm that participants reached that control. Participants stamp, punch, or affix stickers in the box for that control.
- Little Troll program cards and stickers (see below).

Once you have the materials, you must lay out the course and make the map. First, find a suitable place for the course. Try to avoid road crossings, poisonous plants, thorns, high grass, and other potential hazards. Possibilities include city parks, mown fields, woods that are not too brushy, big backyards, and even indoor locations.

Since a String course is only a few hundred meters long, try to design it so that most of the course is within sight of the start and finish. Peruse the surroundings to locate the best terrain, pick an approximate route, and start walking it. As you go, identify more precisely the location of the controls. Be creative in choosing control features that interest children; try to think like the kid you once were.

Once you are satisfied with the course, sketch a map of the area immediately surrounding the course. Base it on an existing map of the area or simply eyeball it—pinpoint accuracy is not essential. Use black ink instead of blue so that it can be photocopied. Include the route, control locations, a legend, and places to punch or affix a sticker for each control.

On the day of the event, lay out the string and the controls. Tie one end of the string to something so that it doesn't blow away. Lay the string on the ground, so that young children can, if they want, hold on to it as they walk. Wrap it around a tree every so often, to keep it from blowing away.

Hang the controls low. If you use stickers, place them in a waterproof bag for protection.

Have a separate registration for young children to keep them from being intimidated by the more experienced orienteers. Timing devices are not usually needed. Have participants color their own maps with normal orienteering colors before they begin. Spend some time explaining the map, course, and rules to the youngsters. Give awards for those who participate.

Advanced String Courses. As young orienteers gain experience, they will crave greater challenges. One way to make a String course more challenging is to leave the locations of the controls off the map. The children must then mark where they are on the map as they reach each control.

Another possibility is to place the control markers just off the string, preferably inside the string. The children use the map to locate the controls.

Map Reading

Introduce the concept of a map as a drawing of the terrain, rather than as an aerial photograph. At first, avoid abstractions such as scale and contours and concentrate on building an intuitive understanding of maps. Further details can be added as young beginners are ready.

Using simple String course maps can be a good starting point, helping to build a familiarity with maps that will carry over to more sophisticated topo maps. Spur interest by asking questions. If the map is colored, quiz them about what the colors mean. Talk about how two places can be far apart or close together and how that difference is represented on a map.

A useful exercise is to have beginners draw a rudimentary map of a room or small spot of land. Once they master that, introduce the concept of scale, and have them measure the room or field and the objects in it, then draw it to scale with graph paper.

Lead beginners out on a nature walk that includes a little map reading. Teach them how to orient the map, turning it until what is in front of them in the terrain is in front of them on the map. If, for example, they are facing south, then the south edge of the map should be away from them. Tell them not to worry if the lettering on the map is upside-down or sideways. Practice keeping the map oriented while on the map walk.

Point out features as you go, and ask your charges to refer to the map and make educated guesses as to what features they will see next.

Thumbing is a useful technique for keeping track of where you are on the map. Fold the map until it is a small, easily held square, and place your thumb on the map near your present location. This makes it easier to refer to the map as you go. Practice thumbing to keep track of where you are.

When you discuss contours, topography, and topographic maps, keep it simple at first. Begin by explaining the difference between steep terrain, with contours close together, and flat areas, with few or no contours. Point out a hilltop with its closed contours, a cliff with its closely packed contours, and a valley with its V-shaped, uphill-pointing contours.

The Compass

Our planet has a magnetic north that is miles away from the geographic North Pole—the north pointed at by gridlines on a normal map. The magnetic north is the reason that a compass works—the needle always points toward that magnetic pull. The difference between magnetic north and true north, expressed in degrees, is called magnetic declination. Fortunately, orienteering maps are oriented to magnetic north, which means that orienteers don't have to calculate declination.

One way to teach children about compass direction is to have them make a simple compass. For both of the examples below, you need only a needle and a fairly strong magnet (most refrigerator magnets will work). Tape one end of the needle to the magnet and leave it overnight. The next morning, test your new magnet by trying to pick up another needle.

Floating Compass. Skewer a small piece of cork with your new magnet-needle so that the cork is balanced roughly in the middle of the needle. Carefully float the cork in a cup of water. Move the cup around the room or take it outside. The needle should continue to float in the same direction.

Swinging Compass. This is even easier to construct. Just tie a long thread around the middle of the magnetized needle and let it hang. Move the thread back and forth on the needle until it hangs parallel to the ground. The needle will turn back and forth until the kinks are out of the thread, after which it should always point in the same direction.

In both cases, the needle will align itself north-south. But which is which? Take your homemade compass outside. Face the sun and stretch your arms straight out to your sides. If it's before noon, your left hand is more northerly; if it is afternoon, your right hand is more northerly. Once you locate north, you can identify it with either the pointy end of the needle or the eye end.

Although children can do a String course without a compass, you will eventually want to buy your children a real compass and show them how to use it. A cheap floating-dial model will suffice on well-marked trails or in familiar country, but if they are going to engage in even semiserious navigation, get an orienteering compass with a rotating baseplate. The magnetic needle of a quality compass is contained in a sealed, fluid-filled, clear vial. The purpose of the fluid is to slow down the spinning action of the needle and provide a quicker, more accurate reading.

Putting Map and Compass Together

When the young orienteer is ready, you can introduce compass bearings in three easy steps (see fig 6):

1. Place the compass on the map so that one of the long straight edges of the baseplate touches both where you are and where you want to go. Make sure the direction-of-travel arrow on top of the baseplate is pointing the way you want to go and not in the opposite direction.

2. Still holding the compass on the map, and ignoring the needle for the moment, turn the dial so that the lines in the housing line up with the north-south lines on the map. Make sure that the N on the dial is oriented with the north end of the map.

3. Leaving that setting alone, turn yourself, the compass, and the map until the red end of the needle points to the N on the dial. The direction-of-travel arrow now points in the

direction you want to go. The number on the dial that lines up with the direction-of-travel arrow is the bearing, expressed in degrees. Although in general it's handy to be able to take bearings, this number is of little use in orienteering.

Figure 6
Sighting With a Compass Bearing

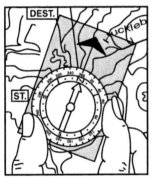

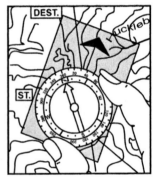

STEP 1: On the map, line up compass with route from Start (ST.) to Destination (DEST.).

STEP 2: On the compass, set the housing by aligning orienting arrow with magnetic-north line.

STEP 3: In the field, follow direction set on the compass. Hold compass level in hand. Turn yourself until needle points to N of housing. Direction-of-travel arrowhead now gives direction to destination.

Navigation, the quintessential orienteering skill that combines the map and compass, will take time for children to master. Teach the skills incrementally, allowing for some success at each step. Navigate together at first, especially on the hard legs.

Once beginners can locate their position on a map, the next step is to find their way on a standard orienteering course. Start with one that has prominent linear features, such as trails or streams, and only one big decision per leg.

Little Troll Program

The United States Orienteering Federation has a four-level program for youngsters doing String and White courses. Called the Little Troll Program, it rewards children for their early accomplishments. Upon completion of each level, the child receives a sticker to place on a Little Troll card. When the card has the required number of stickers, it can be sent to the USOF for a colorful patch and a new card. After completing a level, a child can work for another patch at the same level or move up to the next level.

Please note that not all clubs operate the Little Troll Program. Kids should not expect it without checking in advance with the meet director. The four levels are:

- Little Troll. For beginning children doing the String course.
- Chipmunk. For children learning more advanced skills on the String course. Chipmunks should be comfortable in the forest, understand event procedure, and be able to recognize basic map symbols and colors, as well as control codes (the two-letter or two-digit codes placed on controls).
- Rabbit. For children doing the White (adult beginner) course with some adult help. A Rabbit should know basic safety rules and be able to orient the map using terrain features, navigate paths with infrequent junctions, and consider route choices.
- Roadrunner. For children doing the White course without help (though an adult can follow for safety). A Roadrunner should be able to keep the map oriented throughout the course, make route choices, and orienteer along many paths.

The Youth Committee of the United States Orienteering Federation mails news and information about String courses and other youth programs to USOF member clubs. Further information is contained in the official USOF magazine, *Orienteering North America*, which is available to both USOF individual members and the public. Contact any USOF club member (names and addresses are listed in the Resources section of this book) for details on how to subscribe.

COURSE LEVELS
The White Course
The White course, the easiest standard orienteering course, is usually 2 to 3 kilometers long. It is suitable for adult and teenage novices, and for young children who have developed the necessary skills. Contour reading is not requisite.

Controls on the White course are major features, such as trail junctions, streams, and buildings. Orienteers navigate along trails or streams, through fields, or in other simple areas. Teenagers and adults should try the White course solo or in small groups of two or three. Young children should be chaperoned until they learn to navigate by themselves.

The Yellow Course
Yellow, the first step up in difficulty after White, is usually 3 to 4 kilometers in length. Yellow orienteers still follow trails or other handrails, but the controls are features just off trails or in otherwise more difficult places to find.

Teenagers and adults are usually ready to try Yellow after completing White one or two times. Younger children may prefer to stay on the White course for a while before soloing the Yellow course. They may, however, enjoy doing the Yellow with an adult.

The Orange Course
Four to 5 kilometers long, the Orange is an intermediate course that takes orienteers off trails and into the woods. Controls are found on fairly obvious features or near big features. Compass, pacing, and contour-reading skills are necessary.

Teenagers may be ready to try Orange after a season or two on Yellow, provided they can consistently navigate with some accuracy. Although young children may have to wait until they are older to solo, they may enjoy Orange with an experienced adult.

The Advanced Courses

The Brown, Green, Red, and Blue courses are expert courses. The longest, Blue, can be 10 kilometers or more (by straight-line measurement), placing a real premium on fitness. Orienteers should not move up to the next level until they have mastered the skills necessary to succeed at the previous level. Because of the importance of endurance and navigation skills, rather than just raw speed, people in their thirties and forties often do very well on the longest and most technical courses. Age-group competition, beginning at thirty-five, makes orienteering a lifetime sport.

TYPES OF ORIENTEERING COMPETITION

Depending on where you live, you should be able to find interesting, informal variations in the orienteering you can do. The standard foot or ski competition is point-to-point orienteering, and almost all novices begin that way. But you can also orienteer on horseback, bicycle, canoe, or wheelchair. In some areas, there may even be mall orienteering. As your interest in, and commitment to, orienteering grows, you may want to try some of these alternatives, usually designed for training or just plain fun.

Cross-Country or Point-to-Point. This is the classic form of orienteering. A course is drawn on a detailed map, with controls numbered in the order they are to be visited. The object is to find the controls, in order, as fast as you can.

Score-O. Controls have different point values and can be visited in any order. Usually the controls farthest from the start have the greatest value. The object is to score the most points in a given amount of time. You lose points if you exceed the allowable time.

Night-O. This is either Score-O or point-to-point held between dusk and dawn. Orienteers use flashlights or headlamps. Control markers are usually highlighted with reflective tape.

The Bay Area Orienteering Club's Four Points to Remember

1. Go for accuracy and a minimum of errors. Speed will come naturally.
2. Emphasize map reading. Additional techniques, such as compass use and pacing, will come gradually.
3. If lost, consider the following possible strategies:
   - Find a prominent feature on the map or on the ground that will locate you.
   - Proceed toward a likely collecting feature.
   - Backtrack to your last known location, first on the map, then, if necessary, on the ground.
   - Use a "panic bearing" if provided, or head toward a road and return to the start area.
   - In an emergency, use your whistle.
4. Always check in at the finish, whether or not you complete the course.

Long-O. Long-O courses are 1.5 to 2 times as long as the standard course of the same color. If the standard Green course is supposed to take 50–60 minutes for the top runner in the nation, the Green Long is about 75–90 minutes. Long-O's typically have long legs and complex route-choice problems.

ROGAINE. This is an acronym for "Rugged Outdoor Group Activity Involving Navigation and Endurance." Because the event is so long—6, 12, or 24 hours—and covers so much ground, participants usually rely on USGS maps (1:24,000 scale) rather than on standard orienteering maps. Teams of two usually compete, using a Score-O format.

Relay-O. This is point-to-point orienteering for relay teams of two to four. There are at least as many courses as team members.

For example, in a four-person relay, first-leg runners are each given a map of one of the four courses. (Course lengths are somewhat shorter than usual.) When they finish, they each tag a teammate, who runs a second course. The winning team is the first one to complete all four courses.

A Motala relay, named for the town in Sweden where it originated, is used when space is limited. A Motala consists of three or four short courses, all starting and finishing at the same spot. A single orienteer usually runs all of the courses, returning after each leg to pick up a new map with the next course. All of the controls are set in the same general area, but orienteers must visit them in the order depicted on each successive map. The winner is the one who completes all courses the fastest. Occasionally, teams of two, three, or four orienteers compete, with each person running one or more of the courses.

Memory-O. In this training variation of point-to-point, a map of the first leg only is shown at the start. The orienteer memorizes the first leg (generally not too technically difficult), then sets out for control No. 1. She punches in at No. 1, where she finds a map for the second leg. She memorizes a second route, then proceeds from No. 1 to No. 2. And so on to the finish. As a safety measure, orienteers may be given a complete map in a sealed envelope to be used in emergencies. The winner is the finisher with the lowest time and an unopened envelope.

Corridor-O or Window-O. These two variations of point-to-point orienteering are also used as training exercises. In Corridor-O, the map is covered except for a narrow (100-meter wide) corridor leading to each control; in Window-O, everything is covered except for a small box around each control point. (See figures 29 and 30 in chapter 10.) Both teach orienteers to set and follow compass bearings and to glean terrain information from only a small map area.

Ski-O. This is point-to-point or Score-O competition on cross-country skis. Map (scale 1:20,000 or smaller) and compass are mounted on a board that is worn on the chest. Controls are all located on trails. This is a serious form of orienteering, with national and international championships and the best potential for Olympic status.

Competitive orienteers are quick out of the blocks.

Line-O. Line-O teaches orienteers to follow a precise route. In Line-O, a continuous line is drawn on the map, and orienteers must follow the precise route indicated by the line to find all the controls, which are not shown on the map.

Trail-O. Physically handicapped orienteers are given all the help they need to move along the course, but no help figuring control locations. Courses follow hard-packed or black-topped trails with easy, safe wheelchair access. Upon reaching the control circle, the orienteer sees two to four markers, only one of which is the precise feature depicted on the map. The orienteer must determine which control is the correct one; the participant with the most correct markers wins. These events are often open to the nonhandicapped.

For more information, write to Torsten Eriksson, Valthornsvagen 35, 756 50 Uppsala, Sweden.

Orienteering allows participants to be as competitive as they like. Although beginners would do well to tone down competitive zeal for the sake of skill mastery, competition can certainly make you better. You tend to try harder when you go against others, and it helps you measure your progress. Competitive events are held in hundreds of locations around North America, including regional and national competitions in relay, long, and ski orienteering. At the elite level, the United States and Canada send teams to the foot and ski World Championships and to other international events.

Almost all regular orienteering events have competitive courses and are open to the public. Advance registration is required for nationally sanctioned events, called "A" meets, but not for the recreational courses at those events or for local meets.

See the Resources chapter at the back of this book for both the USOF address and a list of local clubs. Contact the club nearest you for a calendar of events, or consult *Orienteering North America* for a list of upcoming meets.

Map and Compass

I take my children everywhere,
but they always find their way back home.
—Robert Orben

Map skills are at the heart of orienteering success. Maps come in a variety of sizes and types, but they all have three things in common: They are representations of some place, they use symbols, and they use some kind of scale.

You can start by perusing state and city maps, which show the terrain as though it were all one level (planimetric maps). But eventually you must become familiar with topographic ("topo") maps, which use contour lines to show the three-dimensional shape of the land, or topography. If topo maps are too complicated for young children, consider drawing simple String-O maps for them for a while.

Begin by reading the map's fine print. Find the arrow that indicates north. All topo maps are printed with the direction of magnetic north toward the top of the map.

SCALE

Now find the scale, which usually looks like a ruler (fig 7). It shows you how many inches (or centimeters) represent a mile (or kilometer) on that particular map. Orienteering scales are always metric.

Each map is drawn to one, and only one, scale. The scale is the relation between the map distance and the actual distance it represents in the field. Stated another way: It is the amount an area has been reduced to fit on a map.

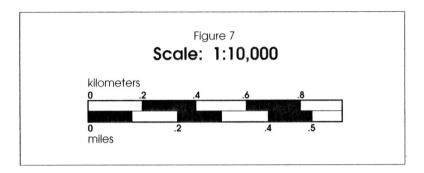

Figure 7
Scale: 1:10,000

The scale of a map depends in part on how much area it covers. On a map of the United States, one inch might equal two hundred miles—or 320 kilometers; on a detailed orienteering map of a park, the same distance might represent one-fourth of a kilometer—or one-sixth of a mile.

Orienteering maps are typically 1:15,000 or 1:10,000—that is, one unit on the map equals 15,000 or 10,000 units in the field. To understand scale, keep in mind that these could also be written as fractions:

1:15,000 = 1/15,000   1:10,000 = 1/10,000

The smaller the denominator or bottom number of the fraction, the larger and clearer the detail shown on the map, and the less territory covered by the same size map. Clearly, then, 1/10,000 is larger, clearer, and more detailed than 1/15,000.

You won't have to calculate fractions to be an orienteer, because most maps have a graphic scale that shows what distance on the map equals what distance on the ground.

LEGEND

Next, locate the legend that tells you what the symbols on the map mean. Symbols are standardized for all orienteering maps by the IOF. With only a little study, you will be able to distinguish between marsh and terra firma, between a ranger station and an outhouse.

In orienteering, we are mainly concerned with five or six types of map symbols:

Figure 8
Map Symbols

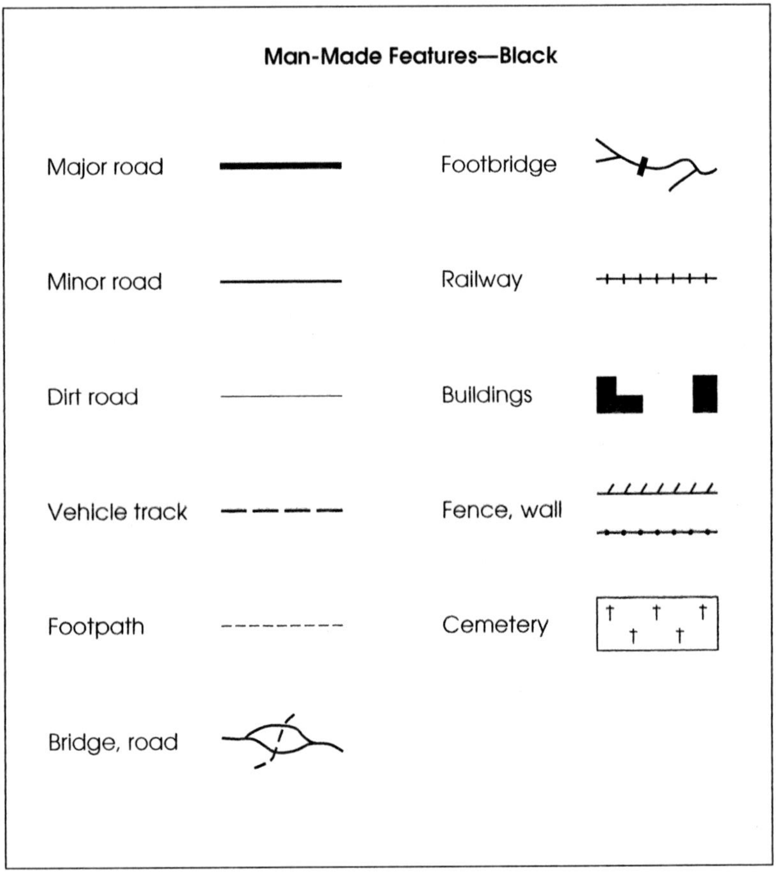

Man-Made Features—Black

Major road	▬▬▬▬	Footbridge	
Minor road	———	Railway	+++++++
Dirt road	———	Buildings	
Vehicle track	– – – –	Fence, wall	
Footpath	- - - - - -	Cemetery	
Bridge, road			

- Man-made and cultural features in black
- Rock features in black
- Water features in blue
- Runnability in green
- Elevation features in brown

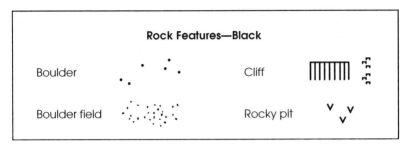

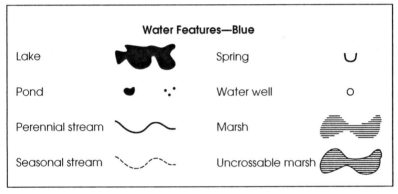

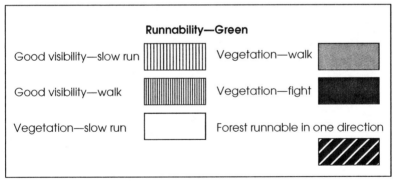

In addition, you will see open land, usually grassland, depicted in yellow, and runnable forest in white.

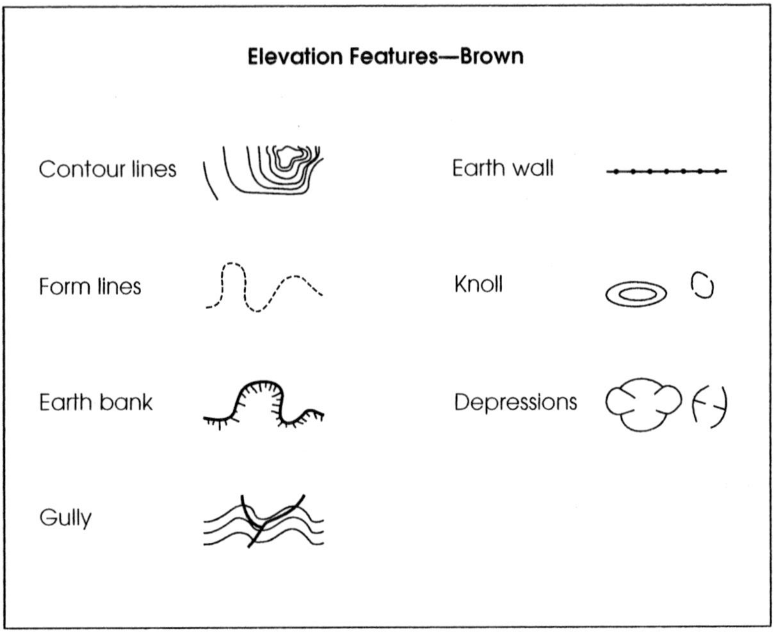

Elevation Features—Brown

Contour lines

Earth wall

Form lines

Knoll

Earth bank

Depressions

Gully

TOPOS

At first glance, a topographic map looks like an incomprehensible jumble of squiggly lines, but it's really quite legible. Here's a way to make sense of it. Imagine that you place an ice cream cone upside down on a piece of paper (fig 9). Your task is to draw a topo map of Sugar Cone Mountain that will depict its cone shape if we are looking straight down on it.

Draw a line around the base of the cone. That circle is the outside perimeter of the mountain. Any point on that line is the same elevation as any other point on that line. Now measure all around the cone one inch up from the table and slice the cone along that line. Put the partial cone back on the paper and draw around the new base. You now have a circle within a circle. The inside circle represents all the points on the cone one inch up from the table.

If you repeated the process, each time measuring another inch up from the table, you would have multiple concentric circles. Those lines are *contour lines*. Contour lines connect points of equal

JOAQUIN MILLER PARK

AND PORTION
REDWOOD REGIONAL PARK
OAKLAND, CALIFORNIA

Mapped by Magnus Rehn, Joe Scarborough, George Kirkov and others.

magnetic north

Kilometers
0   .2   .4   .6

0   .2   .4
Miles

SCALE   1:10 000
CONTOUR INTERVAL   20 feet

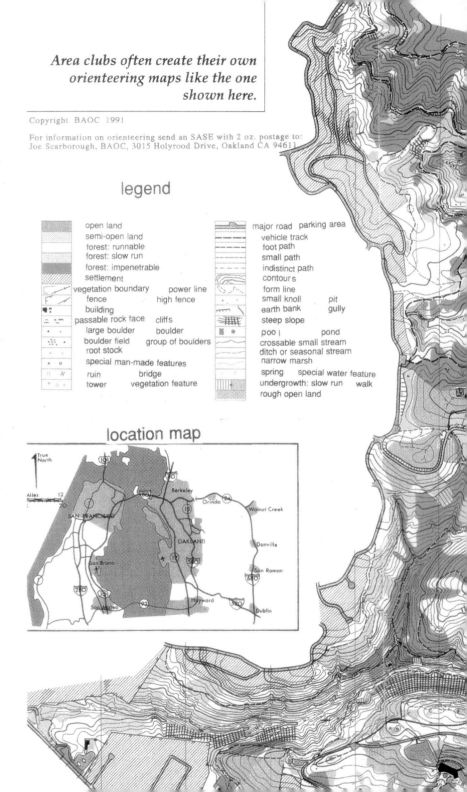

Area clubs often create their own orienteering maps like the one shown here.

For information on orienteering send an SASE with 2 oz. postage to:
Joe Scarborough, BAOC, 3015 Holyrood Drive, Oakland CA 94611

legend

open land
semi-open land
forest: runnable
forest: slow run
forest: impenetrable
settlement
vegetation boundary   power line
fence   high fence
building
passable rock face   cliffs
large boulder   boulder
boulder field   group of boulders
root stock
special man-made features
ruin   bridge
tower   vegetation feature

major road parking area
vehicle track
foot path
small path
indistinct path
contour s
form line
small knoll   pit
earth bank   gully
steep slope

poo l   pond
crossable small stream
ditch or seasonal stream
narrow marsh
spring   special water feature
undergrowth: slow run   walk
rough open land

location map

True North

Miles   12
20

SAN FRANCISCO

Berkeley
Orinda
Walnut Creek

OAKLAND

Danville

San Bruno

San Ramon

San Mateo

Hayward

Dublin

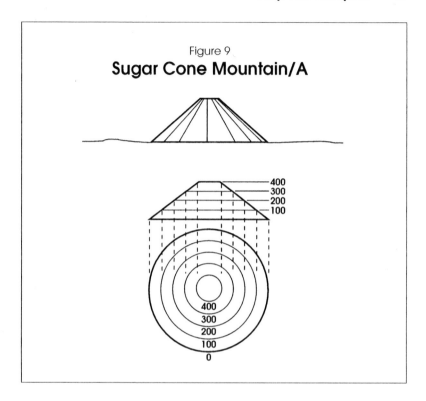

Figure 9
Sugar Cone Mountain/A

elevation, so they never touch or overlap. You gain or lose elevation when you travel from one line to another.

Now let's add a topographic feature to this symmetrical cone. Imagine pressing in slowly near the bottom of one side of the slope. You have created a small valley, or reentrant (fig 10). Now look down at the cone from directly overhead. Notice how the contours of the valley form V's. The tips of valley "V's" point uphill. Sometimes the V's are softened into U's, but the principle remains the same.

Note that if you create two adjacent reentrants, you have also created a spur ridge between them. Spur contours resemble valley contours, except that spur contours are generally U-shaped and point downward.

How can you tell the difference between a valley and a spur, if the contour shapes are similar? The presence of a blue line indicating a stream is a sure sign of a valley. In the absence of a stream, compare the elevations of the contours to determine which way the land is sloping.

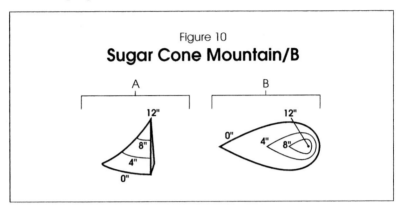

Back at Sugar Cone Mountain, note that the spacing of the circles is constant, because a cone's sides slope at a constant rate all the way around. But what if the cone were asymmetrical? Figure 11 shows the left side of the cone as a ridge and the right side as a cliff. The steeper slope—the same vertical gain over less horizontal distance—is reflected in the closely packed lines.

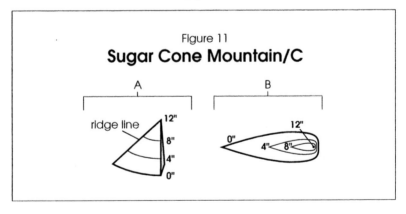

The full-color map found in this book illustrates the following points to help you make sense of topo maps:

- In addition to regular contour lines are *index contours* and *form lines*. Every fifth contour is an index contour, a bold line with its elevation noted periodically along its length. Form lines are dashed brown lines showing small features that are between the levels of two contours.

- The vertical distance between contour lines—the *contour interval*—is always given. If the contour interval is 5 meters, you climb or drop 5 meters if you travel from one line to the next. The larger the contour interval, usually the less detailed the map. The contour interval varies from map to map but is always the same on a given map. A map of the flatlands of Florida might use a contour interval of 2.5 meters; in the Rocky Mountains, it might be 30 meters. It would not do to use a 30-meter contour interval in Florida, where the highest point is 345 feet above sea level; with so few contour lines, the map would not be very informative. Conversely, a 2.5-meter contour interval in mountainous terrain would bunch the lines so severely as to render them unreadable.

- To calculate your gain or loss of elevation, count the number of contour lines you cross and multiply by the contour interval. For example, if the contour interval is 10 meters and your route up the mountain crosses nine lines, you have gained approximately 90 vertical meters.

- Lines close to one another indicate steep terrain—an abrupt drop, a waterfall, or a canyon—while lines far apart show a gradual change in elevation. Because a vertical cliff has elevation change over almost zero horizontal distance, map makers depict such cliffs with contour lines that merge. On orienteering maps they are shown by earth banks or cliff symbols.

- Walk along a single contour line and you remain at the same elevation. Called *contouring*, it can have strategic value in orienteering.

- The closed ends of contour V's show a valley pointing upstream.
- U-shaped contours indicate a spur. The closed ends of the U's point downhill.
- The actual height of many objects—hilltops, trail junctions—is often noted, sometimes with a dot.

Topo Skills Quiz

I. (Multiple Choice) Contour lines that are

1. Evenly spaced indicate _____.
2. Closely spaced indicate _____.
3. Widely spaced indicate _____.
4. Irregularly spaced indicate _____.
   a. Gentle slopes
   b. Varied slopes
   c. Steep slopes or cliffs
   d. Uniform slopes

II. (True or False)

1. Contour lines crossing a stream form V's that point downstream. _____
2. Contour lines sometimes split, intersect, or cross. _____
3. The farther apart contour lines are, the steeper the hillside. _____
4. An intermittent stream is portrayed as a broken blue line. _____

Answers

I.
1. d, 2. c, 3. a, 4. b

II.
1. False. Contours crossing a stream valley form V's that point upstream.
2. False. Contour lines never split, intersect, or cross. However, they may be so close together as to appear to converge, which represents a vertical or nearly vertical slope.
3. False
4. True

DIRECTION AND DISTANCE
Orienting a Map
The simplest way to determine which direction to go is by orienting the map—that is, turning it so that the magnetic north lines line up with the compass needle and the features to your right in the terrain are to your right on the map. After inspecting both the map and your surroundings, twist the map until one corresponds to the other. Once this is accomplished, you have oriented the map.

Taking a Bearing From a Map (fig 12)
To determine the bearing you will follow to get from where you are to where you want to be, imagine a straight line connecting those two points. Then put your compass on the map so that the long edge of the baseplate is on that line. Next, orient the compass to the map by rotating the housing until the north-south lines are parallel to the north-south line of the map. Make sure the N on the graduated dial is toward the north end—the top—of the map. Now read the bearing to your destination on the index line. (See compass section of this chapter for more detail.)

Gauging Distance
With a map and proper techniques, you can answer two important preliminary questions: Can I get there from here? How long will it take me?

Let's say you're going from control to control, and the map tells you that you should follow a trail to a certain point and then cut west into the woods to reach the next control. How far is that cut-off point and how long will it take you to reach it?

As a practice exercise, take a pipe cleaner and bend it to the shape of the route. Put one end at the start and trace the route with the pipe cleaner. If you are following a trail, bend the pipe cleaner to conform to its twists and turns. Using your thumbnail to mark the point where the pipe cleaner crosses your destination, straighten the pipe cleaner, line it up with the map's bar scale, and read the distance. Add a pessimism factor of 10 percent to account for the curves and switchbacks that don't show up on the map.

You can also measure map distance with the ruler edge of your orienteering compass, though such a straight edge measures the distance the proverbial crow flies, ignoring the inevitable zigging and zagging of the pedestrian. Your calculations will be more accurate if you add 20 percent or so to your straight-edge distance.

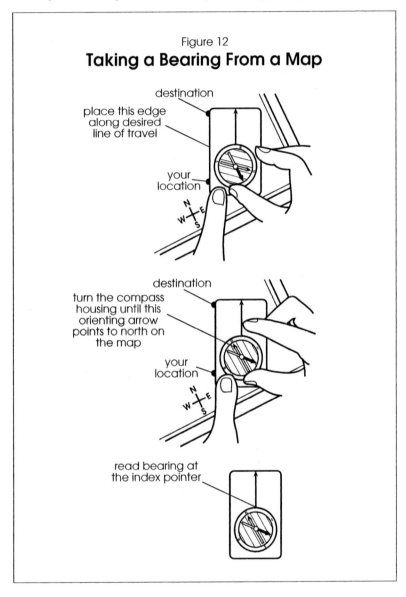

Figure 12

Taking a Bearing From a Map

destination

place this edge along desired line of travel

your location

N E W S

destination

turn the compass housing until this orienting arrow points to north on the map

your location

N E W S

read bearing at the index pointer

Let's say that your educated guess is that you should follow a stream for 100 meters and then cut west into the woods. How to figure 100 meters?

The easiest, but least precise, way is to know how fast you move over various terrain and then watch your watch. The following chart indicates how many minutes the average person takes to cover one mile. You may want to adjust the numbers up or down to reflect your own pace:

Forest	Highway	Open Field	Open Woods	Mountain and
Walk	15	25	30	40
Run	10	13	16	22

A better method of determining distances in the field is by step counting, or what orienteers call *pacing*. All you need to figure your pace is a tape measure and a place to walk. Children, especially, will enjoy this exercise.

Lay out the tape measure in a straight line (or go to a regulation track, where one lap equals one-quarter mile, or about 400 meters). Start at the beginning of the tape and walk a set distance, counting your steps. Now repeat it, this time jogging. To figure your stride length, simply divide the distance by the number of steps. (For example, I take 18 steps to walk 15 meters of level ground. Divide 15 by 18 for a stride of .83 meters, or 2.7 feet.) To be a complete orienteer, you should know your stride length over different terrain and slopes.

Make it easy on yourself by counting double-strides—that is, each time your left (or right) foot hits the ground. After a while, with practice, the counting will become second nature to you, and then you will be able to gauge with some accuracy how far you've traveled.

HOME STUDY

One of the attractive features of orienteering is that you can sharpen many of your skills through practice at home. Called armchair orienteering, home study should be an important part of every serious

Make a list of some places within walking distance of home. Now guess the distance. Check your accuracy by counting steps and doing the arithmetic. Hint No. 1: Count only the right footfall and then multiply by two. Hint No. 2: There are 5,280 feet, 1,760 yards, and 63,360 inches in a mile.

orienteer's training program. The following home-study tips will help you improve your map-reading skills:

- Acquire several orienteering maps (available from local orienteering clubs) and a list of IOF orienteering map symbols (see fig 8). Sit comfortably in a quiet room with no distractions and study the map details, including symbols, colors, and direction.
- As you look at the maps, try to picture how the symbols translate into terrain features.
- Emphasize maps with courses on them. The courses should be at your level or the next level up. If you have blank maps, draw your own course, or have your slightly more experienced friend do it.
- Review the courses you have completed. Study the map carefully to determine which terrain details and map symbols you should have seen and read; compare them to what you actually saw and read. Be honest. You should have seen all the large features and some of the small ones.
- Picture how the terrain looks in different seasons and weather.
- Study other orienteers' maps and courses. Ask questions: What features did they read and use? What map details would you use? What strategy?
- Study maps regularly, at least a few minutes every other day. Try putting them with your favorite magazines by your bedside table.

Map Games

Map Puzzle. Take two copies of an orienteering map and cut one of them into pieces. Mix the pieces, then put it back together. If you get in trouble, use the whole map as an aid. As an added challenge, time yourself or compete against others.

Speed Reading. Spread out a map with a course drawn on it. Look at a small section of the map for a specified period of time. Then cover it with your hand and test your memory of the features you just saw. If you can't remember them all, look at the map again. Start with thirty-second looks at the map and incrementally shorten them. When you can look at a map for only two to five seconds and read enough information for successful navigation, you're a pretty good map reader.

Terrain Study

Map Walk and Map Run. Home study is convenient and useful for gaining familiarity with map symbols, but if you really want to learn how to map read, you will have to go out into the field. Map walks are used in training by the world's best orienteers, but they are especially instructive when you are first learning to orienteer, practicing for a new and different type of terrain, or going out in the spring to start a new season.

Start with a thirty-minute walk, building up to two hours or as long as you're having fun.

The best way to do a map walk is to draw a line on a map of an area in which you want to practice. Use a fine red pen and try not to obscure important detail. The line should wind through the terrain past significant features. Now, go to the terrain and orienteer along the line. Scan at least a 180-degree semicircle, preferably 360 degrees. Try to keep the map oriented; read it often but only briefly—no more than fifteen seconds at a time. If you make a mistake, go back to where you left the line.

The length and difficulty of the line should reflect your skill and fitness level. Beginners should make an easy line that mostly follows trails and fields and doesn't change direction too often. As you improve your map-reading skills, draw more difficult lines—

through forest, for example. Such an intermediate line has more changes in direction but still tends to follow major linear features. Once you've mastered the intermediate line, try a more advanced line, through detailed terrain with many changes of direction. Keep in mind that every kilometer of line usually takes fifteen to thirty minutes to navigate.

In addition to making the course more difficult, you can also gradually step up your pace. Don't break out of a walk, however, until you can comfortably look at the map briefly but often; keep the map oriented; quickly peruse the map and know where you are at all times; map read by thumb; refold the map and maintain position; look about the terrain and identify distant features; move smoothly with confidence, avoiding major stops to read the map.

When you can combine all of that to walk and map read, then you are ready to walk-jog, still on moderate terrain. When you've mastered that level in the same way you mastered the walk, progress to slow jogging, and then to running.

At the Orange stage, get off major trails and try map reading on minor trails, then in open forests, then in dense forests. At the advanced stages, after becoming proficient on the Orange course, try to jog and then run on difficult terrain, all the while map reading.

You can practice different running speeds simply by varying the lines. A long straight line that follows a handrail is ideal for rough (high-speed) orienteering; a line with twists and turns in detailed terrain is conducive to fine orienteering.

When you push the pace in physically demanding terrain, your success is more affected by your fitness level. If it's low, you will tire easily, which will adversely affect your map reading. Moreover, having to concentrate on every foot placement also interferes with map reading. So as you improve fitness and gain confidence, you can concentrate more on map-reading skills. See the fitness chapter for tips.

Line orienteering does not have to be a solitary pursuit. You can go out as a duo or a group, though your map-reading skills will develop faster if the entire way-finding burden falls on you alone. You can also have a friend draw your line or hang a few streamers along your line to serve as checks that you are orienteering correctly.

Essential Skills. As you practice in the field, pay special attention to learning and perfecting the way you:

- Map read on the move. Good map readers do it on the move, slowing when race tactics or a change in terrain demands it. When map reading on the move, hold the map steady and close enough to see. Sneak peeks in the direction you are going to make sure you don't run into anything. If you are farsighted, you may benefit from magnification. Special headsets with magnifying lenses are available; they can be flipped down for reading and flipped up for running. If you prefer, you can carry a small magnifying glass or use the one on your compass.

- Map read frequently. Try to look at your map four to six times a minute. This may be more often than you presently map read, but quick, frequent checks will greatly improve your map skills. During practice, use the second hand of your watch to help you refer to the map every ten seconds or so.

- Read the terrain ahead. Once you can accurately read the nearby terrain and mark your location, start reading ahead. By noting the features and details coming up, you will be better prepared and better able to move swiftly through the terrain.

- Maintain a broad field of vision. Your field of vision should be as broad as the terrain permits. Avoid tunnel vision. Look forward, of course, but also to the sides and even occasionally behind you. In Rough-O, read the map as far as you can see along both sides of your line of travel. The farther you look, the more information you receive to help pinpoint your location.

- Remember features. With each glance, try to remember as much map detail as you can. This will help you orienteer more quickly, since you won't have to stop or slow down to verify your position. Nevertheless, whether in doubt or not, always read the map. It's safer than memory orienteering, and never fails if done properly. To be a good map reader, you don't have to be an expert in memory orienteering.

- Use your thumb. Follow your progress with your thumb. If you have trouble, check to make sure the map is folded correctly and that you are holding it properly.

Map-reading skills may seem overwhelming if you try to master them all at once. There is a preferred order in which to tackle each skill. Limit yourself to those essential to the course color you have reached. Practice the different skills individually; when you feel comfortable with one, move on to another. Be patient, and your skills will improve with practice. If you do not improve or begin to regress, return to the basics to check for bad habits.

MAKING ORIENTEERING MAPS

Map making, called cartography, can be done by one person or many. Because most makers of orienteering maps specialize in one or two areas of cartography, such maps tend to be team efforts. And because the maps are so specialized, orienteers themselves must be involved in all phases of map production except the printing.

The first step is the production of a base map. The base map is usually drawn by a stereo-plotter from aerial photographics, a process called photogrammetry. It shows elevation lines, called contours, vegetation densities, and any features visible on the aerial photographs, such as buildings, roads, and major trails. Field checkers will then walk the entire mapped area, using the base map as an outline. They will confirm all information on the base map and add further detail, such as ditches, boulders, trails, and all other features required to present an accurate and consistent representation of the terrain. They draw these new features on a piece of Mylar with colored pencils. This operation is called field-checking.

After the entire area is field-checked, a mapper drafts the pencil-drawn field work in a form to be printed. The map symbols are color-keyed, and the different-colored symbols are each drawn on a separate sheet of Mylar, using brown for contour lines and other land forms, white for normal forest, black for rock and man-made features, blue for water, yellow for clearings, and green for vegetation. Most O-maps today are drawn using CAD (computer-assisted drafting).

Mercifully, orienteering maps are drawn to magnetic north, so orienteers need not worry about calculating declination—the difference in degrees between magnetic north and the geographic North Pole. Magnetic declination lines are drawn on the map north to south, so that the map may be used with a protractor-type compass. Each map also has a detailed legend of the various symbols used on the map and a bar scale for calculating distances. Most of the maps are drawn to a scale of 1:15,000 (approximately $1/4$ mile to the inch), although 1:10,000 is also popular. The International Orienteering Federation governs the standardization of orienteering maps throughout the world.

COMPASS

Historians cannot agree on the compass's precise date of origin, though credit for discovering magnetism in lodestone goes to the Chinese. Early compasses were primitive—a piece of lodestone floating on a cork in a bowl of water. More elaborate early compasses, with magnets shaped like fish or turtles, appeared in Chinese books in the eleventh and twelfth centuries.

It was not until 1260, when that great orienteer Marco Polo returned from China, that Europe had the compass. Before then, Europeans had relied on the sun and the North Star for navigation. By the fifteenth century, marine compasses were widely available in Europe. Refinement continued into the twentieth century.

In 1933 Bjorn Kjellstrom combined a protractor with a standard needle compass, and the modern orienteering compass (fig 13) was born. It is now the most popular recreational and sporting compass on the market. Although it is more versatile than the old ore-bearing rock suspended from a thong, it's really just as simple in principle. The basis of both is the fact that a small magnetized needle suspended in a housing always swings to point north.

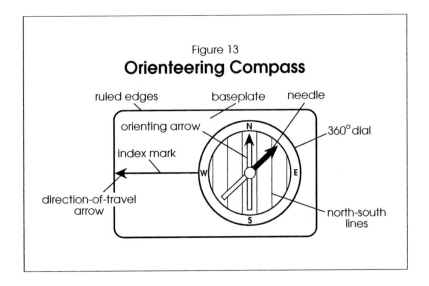

Figure 13
Orienteering Compass

Still, the orienteering compass beats the rock and thong in several ways. With it, you can determine bearings from a map without a separate protractor or having to orient the map to north. This means you can set the bearing while shuffling through nature, and you don't have to memorize anything because the bearing is retained by the protractor setting.

The ruled scale along the edge of the plastic baseplate makes it easy to figure map distances, and the liquid-damped needle reduces oscillation in seconds. The system works at 40 degrees below zero.

It's so simple that an eight-year-old can learn its basics in minutes.

PARTS OF A COMPASS

An orienteering compass is an amalgam of three basic parts, the first of which is the magnetic needle. If you keep your compass away from iron objects, the painted end of the needle always points north. This is very reassuring.

The second part is the housing, which is mounted on the baseplate so that it can be easily rotated. The bottom of the housing is transparent to reveal important features (refer to fig 13):

- Direction-of-travel arrow. This, the auxiliary direction lines, and the longer edges of the baseplate serve as direction lines.
- North arrow. The arrow, usually red, at the bottom of the rotating compass housing. The lines parallel to the north arrow are called north-south lines.

The third component is the baseplate. This is made of transparent plastic, with scales along its edges. Interchangeable scales are available on some models.

In addition, a lanyard, or carrying strap, will help you keep track of your compass. You can loop the lanyard around your wrist with a slip knot so that you won't lose it if you take a fall.

USING THE COMPASS

Orienteers use a compass for four basic purposes—orienting the map, setting the compass from the map, following a bearing, and determining position.

The orienteering compass can also be used to sight a landmark and take its bearing, measured in degrees. This is simply the angle between two lines—one pointing north from your position and one pointing toward the landmark (fig 14). Although accomplished orienteers seldom pay attention to their bearing numbers, taking a bearing is a useful skill that will boost your confidence with a compass. So we'll start with a lesson in backcountry navigation by bearings and then go to the more common uses of the compass.

Backcountry Navigation

Taking a bearing in the field is a simple, three-step procedure:

1. Point the direction-of-travel arrow at the landmark. Hold the compass level so that the needle swings freely.
2. With the baseplate still, rotate the housing until you have the needle in the gate—that is, until the painted end of the needle points to the *N* on the dial.
3. Read the bearing at the index mark. It's nice to remember this number, although if you keep the dial set, you can always read it there.

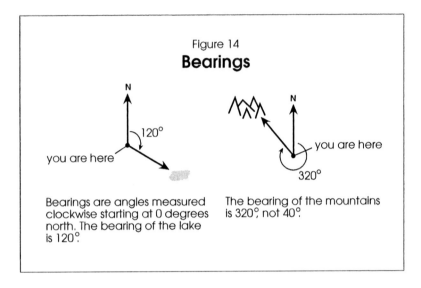

Figure 14
Bearings

Bearings are angles measured clockwise starting at 0 degrees north. The bearing of the lake is 120°.

The bearing of the mountains is 320°, not 40°.

Let's say you already know that the bearing is 60 degrees, but you need to determine which way to go. First rotate the housing until the bearing of 60 degrees is lined up with the direction-of-travel arrow. Then hold the compass level in front of you and pivot your body until the orienting arrow (the one at the bottom of the liquid-filled vial) lines up with the painted end of the needle. The direction-of-travel arrow now points the way to your destination.

Now let's imagine you've climbed a mountain and want to take a different way down. You want to head for Magic Lake, where the big trout live. You can see it from up there, and so you take its bearing, which turns out to be 270 degrees (due west). The problem is this: to reach Magic Lake, you have to drop into deep forest, obscuring your view of the lake.

You could just start out walking the bearing, but walking a straight line in rough terrain is harder than you realize. Better to sight along the direction-of-travel arrow and pick an intermediate landmark. In deep forest or fog, that might mean a target only 50 meters away.

Once you have moved to that target, sight again and choose another target near the visibility limit; move to that one and repeat the process until you reach your destination.

But let's say you come upon a cliff or a bog, something that forces you to leave your 270-degree bearing line. If you can see across the obstacle, the solution is as simple as one, two, three: first, sight along your bearing to some interim object on the far side of the obstacle; second, fight your way around the obstacle; and third, walk to the object you sighted.

If you can't see across the obstacle—the cliff is too high, the fog is too thick—then you will have to count steps and maintain proper direction while you skirt the obstacle. First decide if you plan to skirt left or right. Let's say you chose right (fig 15).

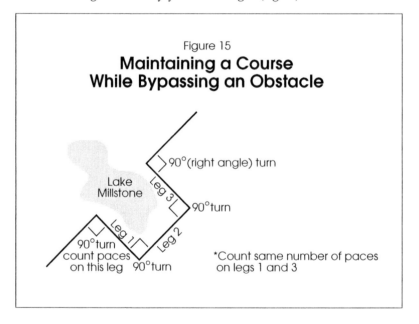

Figure 15

Maintaining a Course
While Bypassing an Obstacle

While standing on your bearing, make a 90-degree turn to the right (the right angles of the compass baseplate can help guide you) and walk far enough to clear the width of the obstacle, counting your steps as you go. Then turn 90 degrees to the left and simply walk until you clear the length of the obstacle. (You are now parallel to your original bearing and can sight a nearby object and use the compass in the normal way to guide you on this leg; there is no need to count steps.) Once you have cleared the obstacle, make a

90-degree left turn and go the same number of steps you took on the first leg. That puts you back on your original line of travel. Turn right, sight a landmark on your original bearing, and be off.

To return home, simply follow a bearing that is 180 degrees from your original bearing. Either add or subtract 180 degrees, whichever keeps your answer between 0 and 360. If you went out on a 270-degree bearing, you will come back at 90 degrees (270 minus 180). If you went out at 60 degrees, you will come back at 240 degrees (60 plus 180). To skip the math, keep your compass set at the original bearing, and return with the direction-of-travel arrow pointed toward your body instead of away from it.

The above-mentioned method of skirting obstacles, though simple, is rarely applicable in orienteering. Joe Scarborough, for example, says that he has used the technique only once or twice in twenty-four years. Orienteers do not generally use it because time is of the essence (they don't want to travel any farther than necessary), and because they basically navigate by map, not by compass. Since unrunnable areas are precisely mapped, you as an orienteer will merely run around them while staying located relative to the edge of the area. Anything you have to run around, you can see on the map and on the ground.

Backcountry Compass Games and Exercises

Games are a fun way to build your confidence in taking a bearing. Here are several suggestions.

Finding Directions (indoor). Stand in the middle of a room and use an orienteering compass to take five to ten different bearings—to a door handle, for example, a table leg, or a picture on the wall. Point the direction-of-travel arrow toward the landmark, turn the housing until the needle lies over the orienting arrow, and read the bearing at the index mark. Assign each bearing a station number and write each station number on two cards. Tape one card to the landmark and one to the spot on the floor from which you took the bearing.

The game begins with each player on a number. At "Go," players use their orienteering compasses to take a bearing to the card that bears the same number upon which they are standing. At the signal "Rotate," players move up to the next number, the last player moving to card No. 1—and then at "Go," they take their next bearing. The winner is the player with the most correct readings, within 10 degrees.

This can also be played as a relay game. On the floor put as many numbers as there are teams. On the landmarks, put as many numbered cards as there are players on each relay team. Each team has one orienteering compass. At "Go," the first player of each team runs up to his team mark and takes a reading to card No. 1. He returns and touches a teammate, who runs up and takes a reading to card No. 2. Fastest team with fewest mistakes wins.

Three-Legged Compass Walk (outdoor) (fig 16). Here's a way to test your navigation skills at a risk of only five cents. Place a nickel on the ground between your feet. Set your compass for an arbitrary bearing between 0 and 360 degrees, say 45 degrees. Holding the

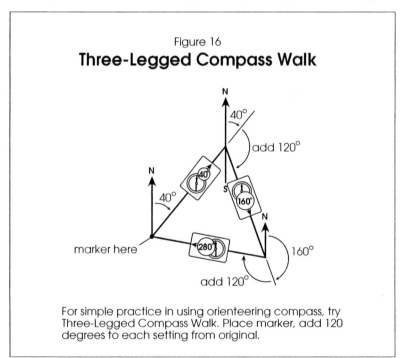

Figure 16
Three-Legged Compass Walk

For simple practice in using orienteering compass, try Three-Legged Compass Walk. Place marker, add 120 degrees to each setting from original.

compass level in front of you, with the direction-of-travel arrow pointed straight ahead, turn your body until the compass needle is pointing toward the *N* on the compass housing. Now sight along your bearing line and pick a landmark more than 100 feet away.

Walk forty paces straight toward that landmark and stop. Now look at your compass and add 120 degrees to your original 45, for a total of 165 degrees. Reset your compass housing so that the direction line touches 165 degrees. Again, hold the compass flat, direction-of-travel arrow pointing straight ahead. Move your body until the needle is in the gate. Sight along the 165-degree line and pick a landmark. Walk forty steps toward the new landmark. Stop.

Add another 120 degrees to the 165, making 285 degrees. Reset your compass for 285 degrees and walk that way forty more steps. Stop, reach down, and pick up your nickel. Actually, if you can even see it, you did pretty well for your first time. Practice improving your compass readings and step-counting until you can "stop on a nickel."

Remember, there are only 360 degrees on your compass housing. Any time your addition gives you a sum greater than 360, subtract 360 from it. If, for example, your first bearing is 270 degrees, your second will be 270 plus 120, which is 390. There is no such figure on your compass, so you subtract 360 from 390 to get 30 degrees, the correct second bearing.

Miniature Compass Walk (outdoor) (fig 17). This game is best played in a forest with minimal underbrush. Attach a series of markers to various trees, each marker with a number and the direction and distance to the next marker. For example, Control 7 might read "Control 7—To Control 8: 225 degrees, 55 feet."

Two people, each with a marking pen, can easily lay out the course. Attach the first marker to a tree and decide on a bearing to the second marker. Write the degree number on the first marker, then proceed in that direction, leaving your partner at No. 1. Measure the distance by your steps until you reach a tree that is suitable for the second marker. Yell the distance back to your aide, who will add it to the first marker and join you at the second marker. In the meantime, you have attached the second marker—preferably to the back of a tree, so that it cannot be seen on approach—and written a new bearing to marker No. 3. Repeat until you have placed about a dozen markers.

Participants, each with an orienteering compass, are started at two-minute intervals. The fastest time around the course wins.

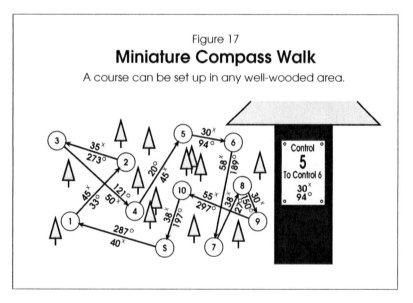

Figure 17
Miniature Compass Walk
A course can be set up in any well-wooded area.

Compass Walk (outdoor). Place consecutively numbered markers on fence posts about 100 feet apart. From one of these markers—we'll call it No. 3—face away from the line of markers and take a bearing. Walk for about ten minutes in that direction, holding the bearing line as precisely as possible. Place a marker there and call it the starting line.

Add (or subtract) 180 degrees from your original bearing to get the back bearing. That is the bearing the participants must follow to reach post No. 3.

Armed with an orienteering compass and that bearing, each player sets out. On a half-mile course, allow a margin of error of 100 feet. Thus, if post No. 3 was the target, give credit to players who navigate to a point between posts No. 2 and 4.

Bee-Line Out-and-Back Compass Walk (outdoor). This exercise is best reserved for those who have achieved some success navigating short distances by compass. Choose an area that you know and one big enough to allow about twenty minutes of travel out—a large city park, for example.

From the starting line, you and all other participants set your compasses for an agreed-upon bearing. You then establish the first leg of the journey in a manner that should now be familiar:

1. Hold the compass level in front of you, with direction-of-travel arrow pointing straight ahead.
2. Turn your whole body until the compass needle is "in the gate."
3. Look up and sight along your bearing line toward a landmark.
4. Proceed directly to the landmark without looking at the compass.
5. Having reached the first landmark (completing the first leg of the walk), refer to the compass and sight toward the next landmark on the bearing line.

When you have traveled the length of time you decided on, it's time for the return trip. Turn 180 degrees, facing where you've come from. Once again hold the compass level in front of you, needle in the gate. Now you either leave the same degree setting on your index line and point the direction-of-travel arrow toward your body, or you add 180 degrees to your original bearing and set this new back bearing on the index line. For example, if you went out at 110 degrees, you will return at 290 degrees (110 plus 180).

Watch your watch. In twenty minutes, you should be back at your original starting point—or close enough to recognize your surroundings.

Orienteering With a Compass

Orienting the Map. This is a basic technique that you perform constantly while orienteering, whether you're a beginner or a world champion. Place your compass on your map and rotate the map (and your body) until the magnetic north lines on the map line up with the north-pointing needle.

Setting the Compass From the Map. This is what you do to obtain a reading for both rough and precision compass work.

Place the compass on the map and align the baseplate (direction-of-travel lines) so that both your present location and next objective lie along one long edge of the baseplate. Make sure the direction-of-travel arrow is pointed toward your objective.

Turn the compass housing until the north-south lines in the housing align with the north-south lines of the map. Ignoring the needle, make sure the north end of the compass lines corresponds to the north end of the north-south lines.

For rough compass work, this process can be abbreviated by what's called *running on the needle.* If your goal is due north, merely look at the needle; if your goal is east, rotate the housing until east lines up with the direction-of-travel arrow and then follow that. In neither case is it necessary to place the compass on the map.

Following a Bearing. Hold the compass level in front of your body. Turn your body until the needle is in the gate (the red end of the needle pointing toward the north end of the housing lines). Follow the direction-of-travel arrow to your destination. If you keep the needle in the gate, the numerical value of your bearing is of no import.

If you find that you always miss to the same side when following a bearing, you may be holding the compass to one side of your body or always skirting obstacles to the same side instead of alternating left and right and taking punctilious care returning to your line of travel.

Determining Position. Occasionally, you will find it useful to locate yourself relative to prominent features in the distance. The simplest way is to ask questions such as "Where am I in relation to that hill? Have I gone far enough?"

You can also preset your compass to a certain bearing from a landmark and proceed until it lines up. For example, I am running north on a narrow path. My control is a boulder among many to the west of the path. I probably will not be able to see the boulder or determine which one is mine from the path, yet I want to continue on the path for as long as possible. There is a large, identifiable hill northwest of the control. To employ this technique, I stay on the path until the hill is directly northwest, as shown by my preset compass, which I now follow toward the hill—and the control.

For a technique called *triangulation,* you take bearings on two landmarks and then plot them on your map. The intersection of the two bearing lines indicates your position.

1. If necessary, adjust your compass for declination or draw magnetic north lines. (This isn't necessary on orienteering maps, but it is on ordinary topo maps.)
2. Take a bearing on a landmark that you can identify on your map, such as a hill or a small lake.
3. With your compass still set at the bearing you just took, place your compass on the map so that one edge of the baseplate touches the landmark (fig 12).
4. Rotate the entire compass until the north-south lines in the transparent vial are parallel to north-south on the map. Be sure that compass north is pointing toward map north.
5. Using the edge of the baseplate, draw a light line on the map that passes through the landmark. Your position is somewhere on that line.
6. Now take a second bearing on another visible landmark at least 30 degrees left or right of the first landmark. Repeat the process above, drawing another line to the second landmark. Your location is the point where the two lines intersect.

    You can usually do this between bearings without actually drawing lines. By keeping the map oriented and by combining it with map reading, you should be able to regain your location.

Once as a ten-year-old, James Scarborough was already at the start of an "A" meet Yellow course before he realized he had forgotten his compass; he completed the course in a time only slightly slower than usual, using only the map.

If you think you may have strayed from your bearing, with no identifiable feature ahead but one behind, you can regain your bearing by sighting on the one behind—a technique called *back bearing*.

If you are contouring on the side of a large, featureless hillside, you can often determine your approximate position by taking a bearing of the *tangent to the contours*. This technique is practiced when you know your approximate elevation and the hillside has a rounded shape with contours close to arc-shaped.

Imagine you are running around an ice cream cone with the tip to your right. Take your bearing by aligning the baseplate with the contour's tangent (direction of travel). Then place the compass on the map, matching north-south lines and noting where the baseplate is tangent to the contours. You are on a line perpendicular to the contours' tangent.

WHEN TO USE THE COMPASS

For orienteers, the compass is a distant second to the map in importance.

Studies of advanced orienteers have shown that even compass experts are significantly inaccurate when they rely solely on a compass. Always read the map first.

Still, conditions arise that demand more frequent use of the compass. These are:

- If your map-reading skills are weak.
- If the terrain is lacking in features or has many similar features.

- If the terrain is complex.
- If visibility is restricted by dense vegetation, weather, or darkness.
- On long legs that cross look-alike features, such as trails, spurs, or reentrants.
- On short legs, or the last part of a leg between attack point and control, when there are few map details, or so many details that your orienteering would be slowed if you read everything.
- To keep the map oriented.
- When you hit a linear feature, such as a trail or a wall, and you want to make sure you turn in the right direction.
- When you cross distinct features in the terrain and want to double-check your direction.

COMPASS CARE

Regardless of the quality of your compass, you will get the most out of your investment if you take the following precautions.

Don't drop your compass or let it be struck by a hard or heavy object. Avoid placing it on a rough surface that might damage the clear plastic base.

Avoid exposing your compass to extreme heat (120-plus degrees Fahrenheit) for extended periods of time. High temperatures can rupture the liquid-filled vial, causing the fluid to leak and making the compass useless. Especially in the summer, avoid the dashboard and glove box of your car.

Avoid exposing your compass to high-powered magnetic fields, especially electromagnets (as in electric motors), which can permanently disable a compass.

If your compass becomes dirty, carefully wipe it off with a soft, damp cloth and, if necessary, a mild liquid soap. Avoid abrasive cleaners, which can permanently scratch your compass, and petroleum-based solvents, which can melt most plastics.

Using a compass at high elevations or low temperatures can cause a small bubble to form in the liquid-filled vial. This is because the fluid contracts faster than the rigid plastic vial, producing a vacuum.

The bubble will usually disappear when the compass is returned to room temperature or lower elevation. If the bubble persists, place your compass in a warm spot, such as a sunny windowsill, until the fluid warms and returns to its original volume. Remember, the fluid in a compass vial serves merely to slow down the movement of the magnetic needle; a small bubble will not affect the accuracy of the compass.

With continued use, the needle may occasionally stick or be sluggish. This is from a normal buildup of static electricity. To remove the static charge, rub a tiny bit of water over the top of the vial.

If your compass has a fold-over mirrored cover, keep the cover closed when not in use for maximum protection.

Getting Better

Even if you're on the right road,
you'll get run over if you just sit there.
—*Will Rogers*

I recall a *New Yorker* cartoon where a sculptor explains his modus operandi for creating a marble elephant—he simply chiseled away the parts of the stone that didn't look elephantlike. That's kind of the way it is in orienteering—you chip away the parts of your game that distance you from perfection.

It's inevitable that you will make errors. The goal is to keep them to a minimum, to correct them as soon as possible, and to learn from them. It may help to be aware of the reasons why errors occur. Some of the glaring ones are fatigue, carelessness, bad habits, poor concentration, previous error, and choosing a course that's too difficult.

When you're tired, your thinking becomes sluggish and unreliable. Fatigue often strikes after climbing a steep hill, after running fast for part of a leg, and near the end of the course.

Great athletes invariably attribute at least some of their success to their ability to concentrate. Unless you have the focusing powers of Superman, you will have to practice this skill. Watch out for fears and distractions that are trying to eat away at your focus.

Errors like to travel in pairs. One error can raise your anxiety level and shred your concentration, making a second error more likely. More often, there is a tendency to speed up and make up time lost in the first error. The result is usually more lost time.

If you consistently make too many errors, you are probably on a course that is too difficult. Drop down to a level at which you finish within 50 percent of the winning time. Set a goal closer to the winner before you return to a higher-level course.

COMMON ERRORS

Here are the most common errors, with tips on how to prevent and correct them.

Missing the First Control

Missing the first control can affect the entire race. The two main culprits are overexcitement at the start and going too fast. Counter early jitters by orienteering carefully until you find your rhythm and become comfortable. Go slowly until you get used to the terrain and map; go extra slowly to the first control.

If you miss the control, return to the last known location, which may be the start. If you can't do it mentally, do it physically.

Parallel Error

This is the confusion of one feature of the map or terrain with another similar feature, such as adjacent reentrants.

Prevention lies in careful map reading where the potential for error exists. Use different kinds of features to confirm your location, especially near controls.

These errors can be tough to correct because you don't realize it was a parallel error. By reconstructing from your past positive location, you can look for the places in the terrain that could have been responsible for the parallel error.

Running Too Fast

Moving too fast is a major cause of losing contact with the map. It's been estimated that as many as 95 percent of the mistakes made by experienced orienteers are caused by not slowing down enough to read the map. Never run faster than you can navigate. As you go faster, you'll have less time to do the same amount of navigation. Before speeding up, no matter what your fitness, first improve your ability to read the map on the run; plan your route, correlate features of map and ground, and determine distance and direction.

Of course, running slower than necessary is also an error. Prevent speed judgment errors by selecting reasonable strategies, balancing your speed with your skills, and remembering the difference between rough and precision orienteering.

The purpose of rough orienteering is to allow faster running—but that can require extra care not to run so fast that you lose track of your approximate location on the map.

Precision orienteering requires slowing, often to a walk, so that you don't lose track of your exact location on the map.

After a speed judgment error, carefully note the direction in which you've been running, estimate how far you've come since you last knew where you were, then try to relocate.

Missing the Control

The objective is to navigate directly to the control feature. You should not have to spend time looking for the control once inside the control circle. The main cause of this problem is the tendency to "fall into" the control by expecting to see the flag once you are close. The result is a loss of concentration when the flag is not where you expected.

You can also miss the control when you don't carefully read the control description, or when your precision orienteering from the attack point is poor.

Prevent this error by paying close attention to the control description and orienteering carefully from the attack point. Navigate carefully, looking for the control feature and not the marker. It's frustrating to orienteer quickly to the attack point but then lose time in the last 75 meters.

Correct the error by returning to your attack point or last known position and trying again, more carefully. Sometimes the error is a result of mistaking the attack point. If this is a possibility, choose another one.

Losing Location En Route

This usually results from poor map reading, veering off course, or moving ahead before verifying the current position.

Prevent errors of location by maintaining good map contact. Refer to the map and confirm your direction often, up to two to three times per minute. Also, stay within yourself, avoiding courses and routes that are too difficult for your skill level.

Correct by relocating; if necessary, return to your last known position and look for a catching feature.

Turning the Wrong Way Out of the Control

In the exultation of finding and punching in at a control, it's not uncommon to rush from the control too quickly and head in the wrong direction.

Prevent this error by taking special care as you leave controls. A 180-degree error—orienteering in the exact opposite direction—could result from confusing the two ends of the needle or from having the map upside down. Lesser errors of direction usually mean poor compass or map reading, or simply going too fast.

Accomplished orienteers prevent this error by planning their exit well before approaching the control.

Correct this type of error by returning to the last known location—back to the control, if necessary—and then continue carefully until you regain your rhythm. If you sense that things are not going well, stop before the error gets out of hand.

Poor Distance Judgment

This happens when you are farther than, or not as far as, you think you are. Because you lack an accurate sense of how far you've gone, you are reading a map section ahead or behind your actual location.

Prevention might include improving your thumbing, pacing, and/or map-reading techniques. Keep track of your position at all times. This is a relatively easy technique to improve by training.

Correction requires relocation. If you are near the control, make a couple of circles around a likely area before bailing out to a nearby catching feature. Keep in mind that people are more likely to exaggerate than to underestimate how far they have gone, so pay attention to the portion of the map before the control.

Poor or No Attack Point

This is a matter of poor route selection that usually results when you decide to take a chance and hit a control from an unsuitable attack point, or no attack point at all. Without an attack point, your chances of swiftly finding the control are greatly reduced, especially in areas of low visibility.

Prevent this error by selecting a good attack point. Correct it by relocation, leaving your chosen route for a better one with catching features and handrails. The farther the attack, the more deliberate your pacing and compass work.

Distractions

Sometimes the presence of others can cause a loss of concentration. Following others can be disastrous if you have no idea where you are. (It's also against the rules.) Don't try to compete with others for speed. The best advice is usually to ignore others, unless their location is an obvious hint to your position.

Know when errors are most likely to occur. Be especially careful not to go too fast for your navigation skills: near the start and finish, in similar sections of map and terrain, when tired or navigating in difficult weather or terrain, if you've just made an error, or when short of anticipated location.

ERROR RECOVERY

The best time to correct an error is early on, when it is small. If you sense that all is not well with your orienteering, take the following steps immediately:

1. Stop or slow down.
2. Orient the map with the compass.
3. Establish your position—that is, relocate. First look at the map and then try to find the features in the terrain. Doing it in reverse order can cause you, however unconsciously, to adjust the map reading to fit the terrain.
4. If you are unable to relocate, reconstruct your orienteering from your last known position. Ask yourself: "What features have I seen? Which direction did I come from? How far have I come? What techniques did I use? Where could a

parallel error have been made?" The answers will help you establish your present position.

5. If you are still unable to relocate, return to your last known location—the last feature in the terrain that you positively identified. If you're not 100 percent sure, choose a different one or go off route to a catching feature.

6. After you have relocated to a feature, check and double check your position and direction until you regain your rhythm.

7. Once back on track, concentrate on regaining a smooth rhythm rather than speeding up to make up time.

Relocation Exercises

Relocation, the ability to determine your position, is the most important skill for speedy recovery. You can enhance that skill with training.

Practice looking at the map more often while on the move.

Find a partner, who takes the lead and the map. After running through the terrain for two to five minutes, the lead stops and gives you the map. Now relocate. You can do this exercise alone, too. Put the map in your pocket, run solo, and then stop and relocate.

Another exercise is to orienteer a course that is at your skill level, but run a little faster than your normal pace. When you make a mistake, relocate.

WINNING THE MENTAL GAME

Talk to athletes at any level of any sport and you will hear of the importance of relaxation, concentration, visualization, "being in the zone." Mental skills are at the heart of success in any endeavor, but never more so than in advanced orienteering. It is the third discipline, after the technical and physical.

Consider this equation:

$$Performance = Potential - Interference$$

Performance is how well you actually do—in other words, results. Potential is a measurement of the best performance you are capable of at any given moment. Interference is the mental static produced by the conscious mind.

As pressure mounts, so do self-doubts and anxiety, two other prime causes of mental static. Again, the conscious mind dives in, usually to provide a litany of advice: "Relax . . . deep breaths . . . look for a handrail . . . an attack point . . . hold the bearing . . . watch out for that root . . . whoops, a catching feature."

With all that advice raining down on you, is it any wonder you're tighter than last year's pants? And the unwanted contraction of only a few extra muscle fibers in the legs is sufficient to affect performance, causing you to expend extra energy and tire faster.

It is clear that a reduction in mental interference will improve performance, even with no change in physical or technical potential. In other words, get right in the head and you can become a better orienteer without breaking a sweat.

Before the start of a competition, you should mentally warm up, preparing your mind for the task at hand. As a beginner, you may simply focus on one or two goals you want to emphasize, such as keeping the map oriented and having fun. Intermediate orienteers will do a little more mental preparation and fortification. Narrow your focus of attention from the everyday flood of distractions to the task at hand. Clean out extraneous debris. As you warm up, organize your thoughts in a way that helps you focus. Have a regular prerace routine.

Many advanced orienteers use two techniques to increase their mental potency.

Positive Association. You've no doubt had both success and failure in the field. Focus on the former and discard the latter. Replay an imaginary tape entitled "My Greatest Hits." Immerse yourself in positive associations. Most competitors have had an occasional great race, an almost clean run when everything was fast and smooth, almost automatic. Afterward, there may be little memory of the mechanics, but the feeling endures of having been in charge and prepared at each stage of the run—a winning feeling.

Visualization. First cousin to positive association, visualization is a type of mental rehearsal in which you conjure up detailed visions of the activity before you do it.

T ips for the Tense

- Nervousness before an event is natural and won't necessarily hamper your performance. Too much nervousness, on the other hand, can lead to anxiety and energy drain.
- Many strategies exist to combat pressure. Consider, among others, autogenic training, mental rehearsal, cybernetic training, meditation, yoga, and biofeedback.
- Do a longer warm-up—activity absorbs anxiety.
- Have a plan for attacking the course. Have back-up plans. Preparation reduces pressure.
- Don't let others decide at what level you should perform. Consider your training, experience, and skills, and set realistic goals.
- If you're on the verge of making an error, stop and talk yourself through the problem. If you have a relaxation cue, use it.
- Keep orienteering in perspective. Yes, you want to do well; no, it is not life or death. Deemphasis may actually spur improvement.
- If other participants make you nervous, avoid them. Keep to yourself until you have completed the course.

As technical skills become more perfected, their execution should become more and more automatic. Rather than going over a laundry list in your head, you will be free to re-create that winning feeling.

The first step is to relax. Use a method that works for you. You might close your eyes and take a few deep breaths. Play a mental videotape of a winning moment, perhaps finding a control or using a handrail. You may see it from your own perspective or someone else's, whichever seems more comfortable. Focus on the finer points of the game. See it as one fluid whole. Hear the sounds of the forest, of your breathing; feel your muscles working in harmony, propelling you across the terrain; see yourself as one with map and compass, zeroing in on your target like an arrow hitting a bull's-eye.

Practice visualization in an orienteering context. Visit an area for which you have a map. Study the map and pick out a target and call it control No. 1. Close your eyes and visualize what the control feature looks like. Visualize the landmarks en route. Proceed to the control, comparing your images of the landmarks with the real things. As you learn more, your images will conform more closely to reality.

Visualization takes dedicated practice, but you can do it anywhere—in the bathtub, at a bus stop—and the rewards can be impressive. I have interviewed and profiled more than forty world-class athletes, most of whom attribute some, if not most, of their success to visualization.

Research suggests that muscles respond to visualization of an act almost as if you had done the act. Thus, the more intensely you can visualize ducking a nose-high branch, the more entrenched the movements will be in your muscle memory. This kind of memory operates almost entirely on the subconscious level, which helps explain how you can do something smoothly but can't explain it to others.

COMPETITION

Excellence does not thrive in a vacuum. As you get better, you may want to pit your talents against others. The following suggestions should give you a competitive edge.

*Concentration and
determination
characterize a tough
competitor.*

Be Flexible. Prepare as much as possible, but don't be neurotic about detail. Every leg is unique, requiring innovative solutions.

Be Realistic. You are only as good as your weakest skill. Be aware of your various skill levels and stay within yourself. If an orienteering problem calls for a skill you have not yet mastered, seek another solution, even if it takes longer to execute.

Stay Calm. When you make a mistake, remind yourself that the other competitors are probably making mistakes, too. Make quick notations of your errors, mostly to avoid making the same mistakes later on the course, but save the thorough analysis for after the event.

Push Yourself. When you confront rugged terrain, steep hills, or dense vegetation, push even harder. Urge yourself on by thinking, "This is where everyone else will slow down, so I will make an extra effort." An aggressive temperament is your ally when the going gets tough.

Be Decisive. Make quick route choices. Route A may be only fifteen seconds longer than Route B, but if you spend thirty seconds choosing between them, you lose time—either fifteen or forty-five seconds, depending on which one you pick. If it's a close call and you can't quickly make up your mind, take the most direct route.

Know Nature. Take the weather and conditions into account when devising a strategy. The challenges of a particular terrain can vary from season to season. Determine direction from nature as well as from your compass and map. Once you are sure which direction you want to go, the sun and shadows offer quick confirmation.

Perhaps the stories of two orienteers who have pursued excellence will be a guiding light.

Joe Scarborough, fifty-nine, is one of the best North American orienteers in his age group. Long before he ever heard of orienteering, he was a runner. In his geography major at the University of California and later in his work for the National Park Service, he dealt with maps. So when he was introduced to orienteering in England, it seemed like a natural mix of two things he loved: maps and running.

He entered some meets in England, returned to Northern California, and discovered . . . no orienteering! Determined to fill what he saw as a shameful void, Joe became an orienteering organizer. "There were nine of us," he says. "But only two of us [the other a visitor from England] had any orienteering experience."

The fruit of their efforts was the Bay Area Orienteering Club (BAOC), now the third-largest in the United States. But starting an orienteering club is more complicated than starting a badminton club. You can't just declare yourself open for business and invite people over to play. The BAOC needed special maps, which meant Joe had to be a map maker. "With the help of two others, we made the first O-map, an Oakland park. It was three colors—today we use mostly five-color maps—but it was pretty good for back then when a black-and-white could be expected."

Joe Scarborough liked making maps, but he loved orienteering. In 1977, after his first year of national competition, he was ranked second in the United States in his age group, thirty-five and over.

He is characteristically humble about that achievement. "That doesn't mean I was the second-best guy," he says. "The ranking system, more primitive than it is now, was based on how many events you won, not on who you beat. Locally I was pretty good, but back East I'd have been down the ladder."

Nevertheless, he steadily climbed that ladder. In 1982 he went to the national championships and won the competition, age forty-three and over, thereby becoming the first national orienteering champion from the West. Ten years later, he was national champion in the fifty-and-over age group. "My goal now is to win it in fifty-five or sixty and over," he says. "The problem is, there are a couple of easterners who are almost unbeatable."

Scarborough admits that he has slowed some in the past few years, but believes he compensates, at least partly, by working on shortcomings. "Experience counts for a lot in orienteering," he points out. "Age groups allow you to stay competitive for years. As you get older, you can look forward to becoming the youngest in a new group, where you are supposedly more competitive. This is a sport you can stay with."

Joe appreciates the sport's camaraderie—he greets friends at meets all over the country—but what he really loves is the feeling of running through unknown terrain and staying in touch with the map: "I've never been through this terrain before, yet I'm able to anticipate what's ahead and go through control after control with zero errors. When that actually happens, it's very satisfying."

A complete run of zero errors is nigh unobtainable, he is quick to point out: "It's orienteering's Holy Grail—the perfect run. No mistakes. All-out effort. But it never happens, at least to us mortals. There's always that little bobble. I usually expect to make at least two minutes of mistakes; I'm satisfied with six, but sometimes it is more. You're always right on the edge; go a little too fast and you risk missing the control. A little too slow and you lose time and possibly the race."

Joe has endured through the usual running injuries well enough to stay with orienteering for twenty years. "You worry about a bad fall, one where you get knocked out with no one around," he says, "but orienteering is remarkably free of serious injuries. I've only dropped out of a race once in twenty-one years, that because of a twisted ankle. I've had lots of lingering injuries: runner's knee, bad ankles, sciatica, plantar fasciitis, and torn hamstrings, one so severe that it did not heal for five years. Actually, the most persistent injury I've ever had was an infected eye, from a twig. It has lingered for years. In the West a serious problem for some orienteers can be poison oak. I've been lucky in that respect."

As a reminder of how lucky he's been, he need only recall a close call: "At a meet in San Diego, I was going down a steep, rock face, when I started to slide and couldn't stop. At the bottom was a pointed rock almost as high as my inseam. I gained speed and landed hard at the bottom, on my feet and straddling that rock, its spike aimed right at my groin. Luckily my legs were just long enough. It occurred to me how close I came to being split in half."

Memories intertwine like the roots of redwood trees, and Joe recalls another near disaster. "Fast down slopes, that's where you can take a fall," he says. "Good runners can cut loose and make up time on downhills. We usually tape our shoelaces so they won't catch on a root or branch. A couple of years ago at West Point I was having a great run. But I hadn't taped my laces and hooked a root. I went airborne and landed hard on my ribs. I was sure I'd broken something. I managed to finish with a fast time, ahead of my Canadian rivals, but the next day I was so bruised I couldn't run at all. Unfortunately, it was a two-day event."

Joe's son, James, a top orienteer in his own right, chuckles in recollection. "Sometimes in training, we carry a tape recorder with us to record what we're doing," he says. "We talk to ourselves, thinking aloud, so that we can later analyze where we're losing time. Dad was recording that session when he fell. Later when we listened to it, it sounded like this: 'Coming down the hill . . . stay on bearing . . . fifty meters to go . . . ahhhh, crash! . . . bang! . . . smash . . . splat . . . ahhhh . . . urgghhh . . . okay, ten meters to go.'"

Father and son laugh at that shared moment, son a little harder than father.

Joe has visited Sweden, the birthplace of orienteering. The O-

Ringen, the five-day annual orienteering festival in Sweden, draws up to 25,000 participants, including Joe one year. "I did it for the experience—and what an experience!" he says, sounding like a groupie who got to jam with the Beatles. "To accommodate all the runners, families, and spectators, they erect entire cities, complete with shops, a bank, grocery store, and sanitation systems."

In contrast, the big orienteering events in the United States usually draw from 200 to 500 participants, which goes a long way toward explaining the Scandinavian dominance. "The difference between Swedish orienteers and North American orienteers is like the difference between North American baseball players and Swedish baseball players," Joe says. "In Sweden, champion orienteers are national heroes. Every kid grows up orienteering. It's the No. 3 sport behind soccer and cross-country skiing. Events are televised. Some think of the orienteer in the United States as a fat old man doing a map hike; in Sweden, it's an elite sport, which trickles down to all levels. There are only about eight million people in Sweden—about as many as in the Bay Area—but they are light-years ahead of us in organization and competition."

Despite the stature of the Scandinavians, Scarborough doesn't shy away from being in the same race with them. "Next year the Veteran's World Cup will be in the United States," he says, upbeat. "That will be my chance to run against the Swedes."

At age fifty-nine, when most competitive athletes have long since retired, Joe continues to run 20 to 25 miles a week. "I have to do the mileage," he says. "I'm neither a natural runner nor a natural navigator. I have to work hard at both to perform at an acceptable level."

Doing 20 miles on a road or track is quite different from running over rough terrain. The former is important for good aerobic and speed conditioning; the latter for competitive excellence. "Serious orienteers have to do the miles," Joe says, "but they also have to do a lot of forest and map running. They have to be able to run the terrain with a map at a fairly constant speed. The best orienteers don't look like they're trying that hard; they look like they're loping, but they are extremely efficient."

Joe's love for the sport seems inextinguishable. "I can see myself competing for years," he admits. "Meanwhile, I'm just trying not to grow old as fast as the other guys."

James Scarborough, twenty-one, glides through the hilly forest like a deer. Glancing at the map folded neatly in one hand, he barely breaks stride. He is one with the terrain. But then, suddenly, he hesitates and stops. His eyes dart rapidly back and forth between map and terrain. He sees a splash of orange and white—the last control! But where is penultimate? He has overshot it, costing himself precious time. It's a bobble of uncharacteristic magnitude. Breaking into a run, he retraces a few steps, cuts left, traverses a hill, and, now seamlessly, locates the missing control. He had suffered a mental letdown, a drop in concentration on an easy control, a result of thinking the race was over.

An hour later, James sits beneath an oak tree, relaxing and restocking calories, fluids. Having blitzed the field on the elite Blue course, he stokes the fires with bread, fruit, and water. Despite almost a two-minute error, his time of seventy-one minutes is eight minutes better than the second-place finisher.

James Scarborough, orienteer extraordinaire.

Lithe, lean James Scarborough, whose delicate features belie his athletic robustness, is a chip off the old block, and then some. At age five or six, he started walking the White course with his mom and dad. At age nine, he soloed his first White course, and at twelve he won his first national championship on the White. "From there I progressed," he says, "always running in my age group in national championship events."

(Juniors compete on each course for two years before moving up to Blue. Competitive age groups for each color are as follows: White—twelve and under; Yellow—thirteen–fourteen; Orange—fifteen–sixteen; Green—seventeen–eighteen; Red—nineteen–twenty; Blue—twenty-one–thirty-four.)

James did not waste his early start. He was able to learn the fundamental skills needed to excel at one level before advancing to the next one. He learned well, winning national championships on each color through Red at least once. "Like a lot of kids, I liked competing, and orienteering seemed like the perfect way for me to do it," he says. "I could run and also test my navigation skills. I thought it was an interesting and worthwhile combination. And unique."

When he was barely nineteen, James competed for a spot on the 1993 United States Orienteering Team, scheduled to go to the World Championships, held for the first time in the United States. James went head to head with the best orienteers in the United States and made the team. Still a teenager, he had earned the right to run against the world's best orienteers.

As it turned out, James was the youngest male to compete at the World Championships. He finished back in the pack but gained valuable experience. "I had good runs on some of the days and did well against other North Americans," he says. "I was encouraged by the whole thing."

James's pursuit of competitive excellence has taught him the pyramid of skills needed for excellence. At the top is map reading. "It's the fundamental part of orienteering," he says. "You have to be able to read very detailed maps. Good orienteering tends to be in areas with lots of detail—contours, rock features, even man-made features. Sometimes an area with lots of trails can be just as confusing as one with no trails.

Since few can orienteer with James, he has learned to O alone.

"You must also excel at compass work and pacing, which help to simplify the map. First you determine the corridor from your compass bearing, then you use pacing to pinpoint the exact location of the control. The sport is intricate. I also run track and cross-country, which require some technique, but nothing like orienteering."

Of course, you not only have to know how to get from point A to point B, you have to be fit enough to get there swiftly. "The real challenge of orienteering," says James, "is to combine the various skills while running at top speed. That's what separates the top orienteers from everybody else. If you are a good runner and a poor navigator, you'll run quickly but to the wrong place; if you're a good navigator and a poor runner, you'll be on course but not move there quickly. You need both intertwined to stay at the top. Oh, and of course, you need the mental strength of an athlete, so you can think on your feet for ninety minutes or more."

In the summer of 1994, James traveled to Poland for the Junior World Championships and to Norway for a big multiday event. He again competed in the World Championships in Germany in 1995. "One of the best things about this sport is traveling and being with other athletes," he says. After a thoughtful pause, he adds, "Orienteers are a good bunch."

In Poland, he and Eric Bone from Washington were the top Americans. Competing in Germany, James finished in the middle of the pack but had solid runs in all three events (short, classic, and relay) and had the best U.S. male performance. Once again young Scarborough was encouraged.

"Now I'm focusing on making the U.S. team again," he says. "The World Championships are every two years, and in '97 they're in Norway. I have to go through squad selection for the third time."

Fresh-faced and slight of build, James carries no excess fat. He burns it in the course of a rigorous training program that includes college track and cross-country—and lots of orienteering.

Already one of the top three orienteers in the United States, James Scarborough has his sights set on being No. 1 and staying there for a while: "Orienteers have a pretty long life span at the top—sometimes ten to twenty years. That's because it's such a mental sport. I'd like to really make a mark for the United States in world competition. It's been done in the older age groups. I'd like to do it in the elite category."

As one of the elite orienteers in the U.S., James has garnered some media attention.

Fitness

Orienteering is a fascinating mix of mind and body. To excel, you must develop physical, mental, and technical skills. If you are new to the sport, you'll probably spend most of your time learning about map and compass. But to compete, and to succeed, against better competition, you'll have to be fast and strong; you'll have to be physically fit.

Competitive orienteering demands a cardiovascular system strong enough to supply oxygen and nutrients to muscles that may be needed for two hours or more. Those muscles must be trained to function efficiently, using aerobic sources of energy, but they also need the anaerobic power necessary to surge up hills, leap over dead-falls, and scale rocks. To accomplish this, tendons and ligaments must be supple and strong enough to hold joints together as ankles twist and turn. Muscles, tendons, ligaments, and bones must be fine-tuned and coordinated with your nervous system, allowing you to respond quickly to internal commands like "Duck!" and "Dodge!"

Fitness, however, is a hazy concept. But it is clear that if fitness is the goal, then exercise is the means. Physical fitness is made up of four basic elements: muscular strength and endurance, flexibility, and cardiovascular endurance. Each is measurably improved with regular exercise.

Proper nutrition is another important factor in physical fitness. Active people expend more energy than sedentary people, and so they need to consume more calories. How many calories depends on age, body size and type, metabolism, type of activity, and level of training. Calories come from carbohydrates, protein, and fat. As a general rule, a well-balanced diet that is low in fat (less than 30 percent of your daily calories) will give you the energy you need to train well. Most Americans get more than enough protein, and those who eat a balanced diet high in complex carbohydrates (sugars and starches found in grains, fruits, and vegetables) generally do not need supplemental vitamins.

CARDIOVASCULAR ENDURANCE

For basic health—and for orienteering success—cardiovascular endurance is the most important element. It is the sustained ability of the heart, blood vessels, and blood to work together to transport oxygen to the cells, the ability of the cells to use that oxygen, and the ability of the blood to carry away waste products. Since every cell in the body needs oxygen to function, this is a basic measure of fitness.

Cardiovascular endurance is enhanced by exercises that force the body to deliver ever larger amounts of oxygen to working muscles. To achieve this, the exercise must be sustained and it must work the large muscle groups, such as the leg muscles. At the beginning of exertion, your muscle cells draw on quick energy sources within their own cells. These are obtained without oxygen, and thus short-term efforts such as sprinting and weightlifting require scarcely any breathing. Such quick, intense activities are called *anaerobic,* a word derived from two Greek words, meaning "without air."

When exercise lasts longer than a minute or two, as in distance running, walking, cycling, swimming, rowing, and skiing, the muscles get most of their energy from processes that demand extra oxygen delivered to muscles and tissues. Hence, these activities are known as *aerobic,* meaning "with air."

Regular aerobic exercise will tune your cardiovascular system, allowing your heart to pump more blood and thus to deliver more oxygen with greater efficiency. Muscles, too, become more efficient, able to use that increased oxygen. This is part of what is called the aerobic training effect. Because your now stronger heart pumps more blood per beat, your heart rate, both at rest and during exertion, decreases.

You should make aerobic exercise at least an every-other-day habit for a duration of at least thirty minutes eash session.

To get the most from aerobic exercise, you should strive for a range of intensity known as the *training heart rate* (THR). To calculate THR, figure your maximum heart rate (MHR) by subtracting your age from 220, then figure both 60 percent and 80 percent of that to establish the lower and upper ends of your THR.

In my case, my MHR is 220 minus 48, or 172.

$$172 \times .60 = 103$$
$$172 \times .80 = 138$$

So while I exercise, my heart rate should be between 103 and 138 beats per minute.

Once you're an experienced exerciser, you may no longer need to take your pulse; you will simply know how it feels to work out at your training heart rate. Two exceptions are highly competitive athletes tracking their progress, and people who need to be cautious because of age, illness, or years of inactivity.

MENTAL FITNESS

Just do it, Nike reminds us ad nauseam, but it's still good advice. By getting out and running or walking, you will derive vast psychological benefits. A study reported in *Psychology Today* found that people who took up running tended to become more imaginative, self-sufficient, resolute, and emotionally stable.

Dr. Malcolm Carruthers and his British medical team found that men and women who exercised vigorously released greater levels of the hormone epinephrine (adrenaline). According to Dr. Carruthers, this hormone is "the chemical basis for happy feelings." Even ten minutes of strong exercise "doubles the body's level of this hormone, destroying depression—and the effect is long-lasting."

Ian Thompson, a former world-champion long-distance runner, has called the link between happiness and exercise "an unvicious circle: when I am happy, I am running well, and when I am running well, I am happy. It is the platonic idea of knowing thyself. Running is getting to know thyself to an extreme degree."

Dr. George Sheehan's seven tips for a long life:

1. Exercise—in work or in play
2. Diet—lots of fruits and vegetables
3. Marriage—(see No. 5)
4. Travel and hobbies
5. Contentment
6. Drinking—in moderation
7. Smoking—don't

Studies reveal striking similarities between the mental states of transcendental meditators and runners. Both activities are simple, free, and allow the participant to "spin out"—that is, to attain an out-of-mind state.

For "meditative" running, it's important to allow enough time—a half-hour at least. To reduce distractions, run alone on a course that doesn't demand constant attention. Run gently and let your mind go; don't cling to one idea.

CAUSE AND PREVENTION OF INJURIES

There are three main causes of running injuries: overuse, lack of preventive measures, and biomechanical weakness. The three are interrelated, since you are most likely to be injured if you have a weak spot that you overuse instead of strengthening.

Weak Feet. Surveys indicate that 35 percent to 60 percent of all walkers and runners have weak feet. If the feet are weak, then the force exerted upon footstrike causes an abnormal strain on the tendons and muscles of the feet and legs.

Unequal Leg Length. Perhaps 15 percent of athletes have this problem. It may cause no symptoms or it may force the shoulders and scapula out of alignment and the spine to curve, causing nerve irritation or perhaps the pelvis, knees, ankles, and feet to rotate abnormally.

Poor Flexibility. Tight or shortened muscles are more susceptible to injury than stretched muscles.

Weak Antigravity Muscles. Running causes back and leg muscles to become tight and overdeveloped in relation to the opposing muscles. Abdominal muscles need to be strong for a pain-free back.

Stress. We tend to stash tension in our muscles, most commonly in our neck and lower back. Relaxation exercises like yoga can help alleviate this problem.

Overuse. Symptoms of serious overexertion are fatigue, chills or fever, insomnia, frequent colds or diarrhea, or localized pain. Each workout tears the body down a bit; without rest it cannot get stronger.

Improper Training Habits and Poor Equipment. Injuries occur when you run too intensely, on hard, uneven surfaces, or in poorly designed or worn-out shoes. (You should change your shoes at least every five hundred miles.)

Foot Care

When you're training to be an orienteer, the feet are the first line of defense. To avoid foot problems, follow the advice of sports podiatrist and *Runner's World* advisory board member John Pagliano: Stretch the muscles and tendons of the foot and lower leg before and after exercise. Pay attention to running form; keep the toes pointed straight ahead. Wash and dry your feet daily to reduce the risk of athlete's foot. Trim your toenails regularly, rounding each one to avoid sharp edges. Choose shoes that fit well, allowing plenty of space between the longest toe and the end of the shoe. Consider adding a pair of cushioned inserts or soft orthotics to your shoes to compensate for the natural loss of cushioning that comes with aging feet. Avoid wearing high heels. Exercise regularly to increase circulation and strengthen foot muscles.

Blisters. The most common foot debilitation is a blister. To prevent blisters, toughen your feet by walking a lot, and go barefoot sometimes. At other times, wear the shoes in which you intend to orienteer, making sure they are empty of dirt and rocks. Smooth out any wrinkles in your socks.

Other Preventive Measures

Test your pace by talking. If you can't hold a continuous conversation, you are probably moving too fast. Of course, fast and slow are relative terms. For world-class runners, who can pound out five-minute miles until morning, six minutes is a relaxed pace. For most mortals, the ideal pace lies between seven and nine minutes per mile. Don't be afraid to incorporate walking into long training runs. Walking can help relieve a side stitch or loosen a tight muscle, and it has fitness benefits nearly as great as running.

Run on a track instead of a road. Most secondary schools have a quarter-mile track. Compared to roads, tracks offer a softer surface and a more controlled environment, and that is good news to the orienteer's most vulnerable joint: the ankle. A sudden bump in the road or a quick jump to avoid a car can mean an ankle sprain—a tear of the ligaments that are designed to prevent excessive motion.

If you find a track, don't count laps—it can drive you crazy. Don't use the inside lanes—the surface there is most worn, and the inside of the track is often separated from the infield by a concrete curb, requiring constant vigilance to avoid striking it with your foot. Alternate direction for variety and biomechanical balance.

Don't gun it on uphills, and beware of downhills. It takes more energy to gain five yards while climbing than it does to gain five yards on the flats. Ground gained in this manner is gained at a high price. And contrary to popular belief, downhills are much harder than uphills on the joints and muscles of your legs and feet. As you go downhill, you lengthen your stride and increase the impact with the ground. Jogging on the flats can create a force equal to three times your body weight; running downhill can double that impact. Unless you are racing and seeking the shortest distance between two points, zigzag down steep hills. That moderates the incline, and hence the impact.

Guard against extreme cold and extreme heat. In both situations, you need to drink before, during, and after a workout. You lose water through sweating and breathing (in the winter, you must warm and moisten the cold, dry air you breathe), and that means you lose body minerals, which can lead to cramps or worse (nausea, faintness, vomiting).

A possible risk of cold weather is hypothermia, when the body can no longer generate enough heat to compensate for heat loss, and it begins to lose coordination.

It doesn't have to be freezing for hypothermia to strike; in fact, it's most common when the temperature is between thirty and fifty degrees Fahrenheit. Far more insidious than temperature are wind and moisture, which can penetrate clothing and remove the insulating layer of warm air next to the body. To avoid frostbite and hypothermia:

- Work out during the afternoon; the sun is your winter ally.
- Wear long underwear and layers of loose-fitting, thin clothing—possibly with plastic bags between them—but wear no more than two layers on the legs.
- Protect genitals by wearing nylon shorts, not cotton.
- Wear a hat, gloves, and shoes with good shock absorption and a little extra space inside to trap warm air.
- Zip up. When you get too warm, you can zip down. Even a moderate workout can make it seem thirty degrees warmer than it is.
- Warm up well. It gets the heart pumping and elevates the body temperature.

Avoid pollution. Because you breathe faster and more deeply when you exercise, you also take in more carbon monoxide, sulfur dioxide, and other pollutants. If air pollution is a problem in your area, work out early in the morning, or in the evening after rush hour.

Avoid sun damage. A sobering 600,000 cases of skin cancer are diagnosed every year in the United States, almost all caused by overexposure to the sun's ultraviolet rays.

If you are going to spend a prolonged period in the sun, the best prevention is to slather sunscreen over the exposed parts of your body. For children and the fair of skin, use a sunscreen with a sun protection factor (SPF) of 15 or higher.

TREATMENT OF INJURIES
Strains and Sprains

Serious orienteering injuries are rare. More common are strains and sprains of leg joints, especially ankles, and hamstring muscle pulls. Self-treatment of such injuries should emphasize RICE—rest, ice, compression, and elevation.

Apply ice for no more than twenty minutes at a time several

times a day. You can use manufactured ice packs, but a wet towel in the freezer works just as well. (So do frozen vegetables in soft packs.) You can also massage the injured area with ice frozen in a paper cup.

Carefully wrap the sprained joint or strained muscle with a supporting bandage to reduce swelling. Loosen the wrap if pain increases or if you experience numbness. Whenever possible, elevate the injured area above the level of your heart to reduce swelling.

Continue with the RICE treatment for as long as it helps your recovery. When you do start walking again, provide support for the injured joint with tape, elastic brace, or Ace bandage. Moderate sprains and strains generally heal in a week or two. If pain, swelling, or instability persists or increases, see your doctor.

Blisters

A "hot spot" is the first sign of a blister. Treat with tape (some people swear by duct tape), Second Skin, Moleskin, or Newskin to protect against further rubbing.

Do not open a blister unless it is the size of a nickel or larger and there is danger of its rupturing or interfering with walking. If you do plan to open a blister, wash your hands and clean the skin with soap and water. Sterilize a pin or needle over a flame, holding the end of the pin with a cloth, then let it cool. Puncture the base of the blister, not the center, and let it drain from the pinprick. Apply an antibiotic ointment, then cover with a light bandage, a piece of gauze, or a thin foam pad with a hole in the center.

Check daily for signs of infection—reddening, swelling, or pus. See a doctor if infection occurs.

Heel Bruise

Caused by excessive, perhaps unaccustomed road work with poor heel cushioning, or by coming down hard on a sharp object, this can be a nagging injury. The athlete typically has about $1\,1/2$ square inches of tenderness on the undersurface of the heel bone. The pain may persist all through the run or disappear as you heat up.

Treatment includes wearing well-cushioned training shoes with firm heel pads (not thin foam rubber). Move your training

The Road Runners Club of America offers these safety tips:

- Carry identification, including medical information. Do not wear jewelry.
- Carry a quarter for a phone call.
- Run with a partner.
- Leave word of your route, and alter it occasionally. Know where telephones and open businesses are.
- Avoid unpopulated areas, overgrown trails, unlit areas at night, and parked cars.
- Don't wear a headset. Stay alert.
- Ignore verbal harassment.
- Run against traffic.
- If you must run before dawn or after dark, wear reflective material or carry a light.
- Carry a whistle or other noisemaker.

venue to dirt, grass, or track, and reduce the distance by 30 percent for ten days.

Heat Illness

Drinking plain water is the best way for the average person to replace lost fluids. Excessive loss of sodium and potassium (electrolytes) occurs only after a severe and prolonged sweat.

If a person is suffering heat cramps, try rest, gentle massage, stretching, and lots of drinking. Now is the time to replace minerals with a sport drink. Ice comforts painful muscles and reduces inflammation. For the common calf cramp, straighten out and support the affected leg, grasp the foot at the toes, and pull slowly and gently. Never pound or twist a cramping muscle.

If the illness has progressed to heat exhaustion, where the person may be dizzy but heart rate and temperature are normal, use the same treatment but also apply wet cloths to the victim and fan vigorously. When the victim feels better, activity can be resumed.

Heatstroke is an emergency. Body temperature is between 102

and 104 degrees Fahrenheit; the skin is hot and usually dry; pulse and respiration rate are elevated.

Get the victim in the shade, and sponge him down, especially around the armpits, groin, and neck. Give liquids only if the victim is conscious and able to swallow. Do not administer aspirin or stimulants. After the condition has stabilized, get the victim to a doctor as soon as possible.

EMERGENCY MEDICINE

Although life-threatening emergencies seldom occur in orienteering, it is possible that emergency medicine may be needed, as shown in the preceding discussion of hypothermia. In the absence of someone trained in first aid and/or cardiopulmonary resuscitation (CPR), you should know how to contact the emergency support services in the area.

IRRITATING AILMENTS
Mosquito Bites

Mosquitoes are prolific and voracious, and willing to give their life for one last shot at your juicy self. You have to admire that kind of dedication.

The first rule in mosquito country is to know your limitations. You can't kill or outrun them all. Lured by your warmth and expired carbon dioxide, they move in for the attack. Even if they don't strike (only the females bite), their incessant whining in your ears may drive you to take up indoor sports.

The second rule, for me, is to use a chemical repellent containing DEET (diethyl metatoluamide). The powerful DEET is absorbed through the skin—48 percent of an application is absorbed within six hours. This means it can cause side effects. The most common side effect is a rash, but occasionally anxiety, behavioral changes, lethargy, and mental confusion have been reported. If you agree with me that it's worth the risk, apply it sparingly to skin and liberally on clothes. After applying DEET, wash your hands or keep them away from your eyes and mouth. With young children, don't use a repellent with more than about a 30 percent concentration of DEET. If you prefer an alternative to DEET, try Natrapel, which contains citronella.

If you insist on being bitten, don't scratch. Always an attraction to mosquitoes, I used to be a mad scratcher, which resulted in quarter-size welts followed by hideous scabs followed by scars. Eventually, I learned that if I can get through the first half-hour without scratching, the welt goes away. Anti-itch medicines may help you resist.

Poison Oak/Ivy/Sumac

Poison oak, ivy, and sumac contain an irritant called urushiol, a sap found in the roots, stems, and leaves. The plant must be touched, bruised slightly, to release urushiol; you can't get a rash from just being in the neighborhood.

The best way to escape the wrath of urushiol is to know what the plants look like and stay away from them. Keep in mind the ditty "Leaves of three, let it be" (though if you take that too literally, you'll miss out on some good berries). The poison plants may cling to the ground or grow up the trunks of trees or along fences. They may look like shrubs, bushes, small trees, or vines. Leaves may be dull or glossy with sawtoothed or smooth edges. In autumn, the leaves may turn orange; in summer, poison ivy has white berries.

If you think you've touched poison plants, put on clean gloves and carefully remove your clothing. Wash everything in strong detergent. Wipe off your shoes. Wash your body with soap and water. (You might first try rubbing with an anti–poison ivy lotion such as Tecnu.)

If you develop an itchy rash, try not to scratch. Scratching won't cause the rash to spread, but it can lead to infection. The blisters don't contain urushiol, so you can't pass the rash to another person. However, if you have the oil on your body before the rash develops, you can pass it by touching someone.

Cold saltwater compresses, cool baths, calamine, baking soda, and over-the-counter cortisone cream offer relief. The best product I've found for drying up the blisters is Derma Pax. But even if you do nothing, you'll probably be rid of all traces in less than three weeks.

Be happy. With thousands of plant species in North America, it could be worse.

Training

We're all in this alone.
—Lily Tomlin

GENERAL TRAINING PRINCIPLES

Whether you're a nationally ranked Blue-course orienteer or a White-course beginner, you should have some kind of fitness program. Your approach and your rate of progress will depend on many factors, since you are a unique individual. Your potential is genetically determined and environmentally realized.

Age and physical maturation are also factors. Prepubescents must channel much of their energy into growth. Many children's coaches limit strength training and prohibit their charges from running more than five kilometers in training or competition.

Children lack the experience necessary to accurately assess their exertion level. They are also at greater risk for heat-related illnesses. With their smaller body surfaces, they cool more slowly than adults.

Your current fitness level will greatly affect your rate of improvement. If you're out of shape when you start, you will progress rapidly. Once you become more fit, greater effort is required to see slight improvements. Keeping track of accomplishments—whether it's how much weight you lift or how fast you run the mile—can provide the positive reinforcement needed to persevere.

Lifestyle can also affect your ability and willingness to train. Working a job sixty hours a week will preclude a serious training regimen. Stress can also cut into your workout. A diet rich in fat and low in complex carbohydrates and vitamins will probably not support the energy level required to train. Long-term sleep deficit will have the same effect.

To receive maximum benefits from exercise, you must make it a long-term habit. Make a firm commitment to set aside at least thirty minutes every other day for exercise. On a weekly basis, that's about two hours out of every 168, or a mere 1.2 percent of your time. The other 98.8 percent of your time will be greatly enhanced by that small investment in exercise.

Make a weekly schedule. Block in your work time, sleep time, eating time, and other needs. Now fit in those two hours of exercise. Find the time that's best for you; make a date with yourself.

Walking

Walking is a great way to start. A simple, safe, and inexpensive form of recreation, it is also an effective means to sustain a lifelong exercise program. Walking briskly—at least $3^1/2$ miles per hour—offers almost the same aerobic benefits as jogging and burns only 10 percent to 20 percent fewer calories. Walking builds leg muscles, strengthens bones, curbs the appetite, and exercises the back and feet.

Start by getting the right footwear. Each foot hits terra firma almost a thousand times a mile, so you want to do it right. Don't walk long distances in soft, shapeless shoes. Walking shoes should have a rigid arch as well as some cushioning in the heel and ball of the foot.

Incorporate walking into your daily routine. Don't ride when you can walk. If you take public transportation, get off a few stops early and walk to your destination. Take the stairs instead of the elevator. Infuse your walking program with variety. Walk different routes with different people. Vary your pace. Add hills, which will further boost the aerobic benefits. Don't accept the two biggest excuses for staying home: time and weather. Make time by elevating exercise from the bottom of your personal priority list. If the weather is severe, walk in a climate-controlled environment. Many malls have walking programs sponsored by the American Heart Association.

If you're inactive but healthy, start with mile-long walks at a pace of 3 mph five times a week. Gradually increase your distance to at least 3 miles and your pace to 4 mph. As you get used to walking, start carrying a backpack with a little weight in it. As fitness improves, add more weight.

Consider the following twelve-week walking plan to help you get started and keep going. Walk three days a week for the amount of time shown. At the end of twelve weeks, you can stay at the level you've reached or continue to increase your output.

MINUTES PER DAY SPENT WALKING

Week	Day 1	Day 2	Day 3
1	10	10	10
2	12	12	16
3	15	15	20
4	15	20	25
5	20	25	35
6	30	35	45
7	35	35	50
8	40	40	60
9	45	45	60
10	45	45	70
11	45	45	80
12	45	45	90

Source: *Men's Health* magazine

Hiking

Yes, of course, hiking is walking, but with important differences. Hiking takes place on trails or cross-country, not on roads. It is rambling through the woods or over hill and dale, and if you're going to be an orienteer, you'll have to do a lot of hill and dale.

Hiking, open to all ages and abilities, provides a wide range of challenges. Whether you hike alone or with others, you can get a first-rate workout. Hiking a rough but level trail expends about 50 percent more energy than walking on a paved road. And hiking

> Hills make all men brothers.
> —Dr. George Sheehan

uphill further boosts the caloric expenditure and aerobic benefits. Ascending a 14-degree slope requires almost four times the effort of walking on level ground. A 150-pound person hiking at a moderate pace for eight hours over varied terrain will burn about 3,500 calories—a thousand more than a good runner burns doing a marathon. Add a backpack, and that total increases.

There are also considerable psychological benefits to hiking. Passing through nature relaxes the mind, stimulates creativity, and helps you shed stress. Force-feeding yourself all that fresh air doesn't hurt, either.

Running

If you're going to be an accomplished orienteer, you will have to run. How far and how fast depends on genetics and your motivation to train.

Take that first step and take it regularly—at least every other day. Establish a routine—a happy one—and when you get out of it, gently prod yourself back. Even two weeks of inactivity can measurably reduce your fitness level, an effect called "detraining." If you are sidelined with an injury that prevents you from running, use the stationary bicycle, or the stair-stepper, or something else.

Preparation

Give yourself time to prepare physically and mentally for your walks or runs. Avoid feeling rushed. Look forward to having fun—which may be more likely if you leave your watch at home. According to Jim Fixx, "Stopwatch runners tend to be haunted, driven souls."

Studies show that the way you imagine an event may shape the way the event plays out. See yourself excelling. See your workout in as much detail as possible—the course, the scenery, the competition; feel the pain, the joy, the weather. Do this regularly, and it will become easier. Most successful athletes use visualization.

Few people know how to take a walk. The qualifi-
cations . . . are endurance, plain clothes, old shoes,
an eye for nature, good humor, vast curiosity, good
speech, good silence and nothing too much.
                                    —Ralph Waldo Emerson

Try these four pre-workout visualization exercises: Imagine all
the tension leaving your legs; now imagine them free and loose.
Imagine your body as a finely tuned, well-oiled machine; that also
helps later when dealing with pain. Picture yourself feathery light
on your feet. Finally, if you know your course, see yourself passing
several landmarks along the way and feeling great. It might be
helpful to create a self-fulfilling prophecy by repeating a little chant
like "I feel so good, I could run forever."

Stretch regularly. This is somewhat controversial; David Hor-
ton, who holds the speed record for the 2,140-mile Appalachian
Trail, is one of those who skip stretching and immediately hit the
trail, albeit at a slower-than-normal pace. But most experts still
make a case for light stretching—after a warm-up and before the
main event, as well as after the main event—especially for problem
areas such as hamstrings, calves, and Achilles tendons.

If you stretch, do it right. Don't bounce. Stretch to the point
where it is difficult to go further, and then relax into the stretch.
Exhale and hold the stretch about fifteen seconds. Repeat. If there is
sharp pain with the stretch, back off.

Sleep regularly and well, but don't worry about it if you don't.
In the short run, the amount of sleep you get affects physical performance very little; the biggest impact is psychological.

In the long run, the average person requires eight hours of sleep
every twenty-four hours, and virtually everybody needs between
four and ten. How much sleep you need is determined mostly by
genetics, but you can improve the quality of your sleep. Classic bro-
mides still work: drink warm milk, take a warm bath before bed

time, and avoid regular use of sleeping pills. Of course, regular exercise also makes you a better sleeper.

Leave negative emotions in the locker room. A bad day at home or work can easily spill over, causing a bad workout. Although some people can effectively fuel exercise with anger, negative emotions interfere with the quality of most people's workouts.

Don't eat a lot right before hitting the road. This is more critical for runners than for walkers, but both would do well to exercise no sooner than two to four hours after eating. Eating just before exercise recruits blood for digestion when it's needed to flush out the lactic acid that builds up in the muscles during a high-intensity workout.

Set goals. Realistic short- and long-term goals will serve as both a motivational tool and a way of measuring progress.

Prepare for hot weather, the pedestrian's greatest meteorological misery. Consider making these summertime adjustments:

1. Drink water often.
2. Hit the road at dawn or dusk.
3. Go shorter and slower.
4. Stay on the grass and off hot pavement.
5. Increase stretching and icing.
6. Train indoors.
7. Break up the routine with a swim or bike ride.
8. Eat cool, light foods with an emphasis on carbohydrates (which help muscles hydrate).
9. Visualize cool.
10. Head north.

Training Techniques

Moving. It's important to move naturally. Each person has his or her own distinctive natural style and carriage. Jim Ryun, former world record holder in the mile, was a "head-roller"; four-time Olympic gold medalist Emil Zatopek is said to have "boxed his way through a race."

Still, there are some standards to shoot for. In general, you should keep your body erect, your shoulders even, and your head up. Your hips, knees, and ankles should stay relaxed. Use the arms for balancing and power, but push from the shoulders and don't exaggerate the arm swing. The wrists should be fairly firm, the elbows bent but not held tightly against the chest. The hands should be in a relaxed C shape, not tightened fists, though occasionally shaking tension from the fingertips can be effective.

You should land first on the outside edge of the foot and roll inward, with the rolling action cushioning the impact. Sprinters contact the ground high on the ball of the foot; middle-distance runners hit on the metatarsal arch; long-distance runners, joggers, and walkers strike heel first. If you walk or jog on your toes, you risk shin splints, strained calf muscles, and Achilles tendon problems.

Breathing. Breathe naturally. As you move faster, don't be afraid to breathe through your mouth. Gulp in all the air you can.

Changing the Slope. Avoid striding too long on uneven ground with the same slant. Banked tracks or roads that tilt near the curb can alter the biomechanics of your gait. If you must train on slanted surfaces, change directions after a while to avoid a repetitive imbalance. Do hill work. It offers the benefits of speed work in a more appealing setting than a track. It strengthens the quadriceps and buttocks without the heavy pounding of sprinting.

Work for gradual improvement. Don't go too far or too fast in the beginning, lest you succumb to injury or burnout. Work up to greater distances.

Sticking With It. In the absence of injury, cover the distance you set out to do. If you intend to do 2 miles, do 2 miles even if you have to reduce your usual pace. This will help toughen the mind and teach you to endure the hard runs as well as the easy ones. As Jim Fixx said, "If you quit when training goes badly, you only learn how easy it is to avoid discomfort."

For the long term, remember that variety will help you stay with the program. Join a walking club; subscribe to a running magazine; take a day off; explore a new trail.

TRAINING FOR ORIENTEERING

The aim of new orienteers starting to train should be to reach their maximum potential. Whether that level is club, regional, national, or international, train to bring out the best in yourself. Obviously, everyone cannot be world champion—or even club champion. What almost everyone can do, however, is to reach a competitive level that brings them satisfaction and pride.

Fortunately, orienteering offers a series of progressively more challenging courses that can serve as stepping-stones for the upward-advancing orienteer. With something to aim for at every stage—faster times, fewer mistakes, less fatigue—the orienteer stays motivated.

I n order to plan a training program, or have a coach plan one for you, you must first consider:
- Your current level of fitness and training
- Your knowledge of and ability to use orienteering techniques
- Your motivation and goals in orienteering
- Your available time and facilities
- Your previous training experience

To direct training toward a particular sport, it is first necessary to consider what that sport demands of its competitors. Competitive orienteers must be able to:

1. Run fast for distances varying from 100 meters to 1 kilometer, with only short recovery periods in between bursts, and sustain it for the entire course.
2. Run fast over rough, sloping ground.
3. Run fast while not thinking about running in order to leave the mind free to solve navigation problems.

Before we delve into the aerobic and anaerobic training necessary to achieve those goals, let's start with a warm-up.

Warm-up

Plan on ten to fifteen minutes of activity, which gradually increases in intensity. The ideal warm-up heats up muscles and connective tissues, making them more supple and resistant to injury. A typical warm-up phase might include a brisk walk for two to five minutes, followed by stretching from head to toes. Stretch to the point of discomfort and hold for about fifteen seconds; avoid ballistic stretching. Alternate muscles that flex with those that extend. Work for symmetry.

EXAMPLES OF STRETCHES

Back and Neck
- Bent-knee toe touches
- Stand and arch
- Side bends
- Twist upper back
- Flex and extend neck
- Bend neck side to side
- Rotate chin over shoulder

Arms
- Reach vertically—both arms
- Reach forward—both arms
- Arm circles—both arms
- Chest stretch—both arms

Legs
- Groin stretch
- Quad stretch, standing
- Hamstring stretch
- Calf stretch, both bent and straight knee
- Raise up on toes
- Ankle rolls, not weight bearing

Training to Last the Course

The first goal for beginners and many juniors is simply to be able to run the entire course. Doing quick bursts will come later.

Three types of training will help you reach this first objective: long slow distance, intervals/fartlek, and downhill runs.

Long Slow Distance (LSD). Developed by Dr. Ernst van Aaken and popularized by *Runner's World* editor Joe Henderson, LSD conditions the cardiovascular and respiratory systems and hence raises your fitness base. It is also less likely than fast running to injure tendons and muscles. The only disadvantage is that it doesn't teach you how to relax when moving at the fast pace needed for racing.

Nevertheless, LSD is an important starting point as it provides the aerobic base that allows you to benefit from other types of training. It accustoms the body to a fairly high level of exercise sustained for a considerable length of time. It also teaches you to run in a relaxed, comfortable manner, expands the capillary network and blood flow to the muscles, and burns more than one hundred calories per mile. LSD should dominate the training schedule when competition is not imminent, and it is then that any increases in training should take place.

Emphasize comfortable running, with no oxygen debt, at a pace that allows you to converse. If you are unfit, start out slowly doing short distances. As you become fitter, you will gradually go faster and longer. Avoid too much too early, which is a blueprint for injury. A rule of thumb is for beginners to progress no more than 5 percent each week. Fit orienteers should regularly cover a distance greater than the course on which they plan to compete.

Although LSD is an important starting point, it alone does not a training regimen make. Some orienteers prefer to do only LSD training because it's easier and they like it; however, they will not reach their full potential by limiting themselves to steady running. LSD can provide a good fitness base but does not develop speed.

Make your aerobic training fun by mixing in long-distance biking, swimming, or cross-country skiing. When conditions force you inside, you can aerobicize on stair-steppers, ski machines, rowing machines, treadmills, or stationary bikes.

Intervals/Fartlek. After developing an aerobic base, begin to insert bursts of speed into your rambles. If you intend to do it in competition, you had better do it in practice. The accepted way to boost your body's cardiovascular system is by exercising steadily for twenty to thirty minutes three to five times a week. But recent research indicates that you may be able to get in shape faster with interval training—short bursts of intense activity, each followed by partial recovery periods.

Interval principles can be applied to almost any exercise, but orienteers should emphasize repeated hard runs with recovery periods—intervals—of relaxed jogging or walking in between. Vary the duration of the intervals to prepare for courses of different lengths and hills of different heights.

During the intense phases, your heart rate should reach 80 percent of its maximum (up to 90 percent if you are in top condition). During the recovery periods, don't let your heart rate dip below 60 percent of its maximum. If you are over forty-five, out of shape, or have a medical condition that restricts your ability to exercise, consult your doctor about interval training.

One method of doing intervals is called *fartlek,* a Swedish word for "speed play." Although it's ideal for a group of three to five of fairly equal ability, you can also do it in pairs. The leader runs along at a comfortable pace until, at his choosing, he suddenly speeds up for thirty or more seconds, with the others in pursuit. He then slows, and a new leader moves to the front. Each leader should have two or three chances to set the pace.

Interval training helps to develop your ability to run anaerobically, develops a sense of pace, and offers needed variety. Intervals can be run on a variety of surfaces—tracks, grass, sand—and no formal layout is necessary.

Strict interval training seems too formal to some people, but it can rapidly improve orienteering performance. Vary the lengths of the bursts and cut down recovery to simulate orienteering. Count steps or use a track to confirm your distances.

A typical orienteer's interval session might look like this (all distances are in meters): 50 fast, 50 jog; 100 fast, 100 jog; 200 fast, 200 jog; 400 fast, 400 jog; 600 fast, 600 jog; 800 fast, 800 jog; 600 fast, 600 jog; 400 fast, 400 jog; 200 fast, 200 jog; 100 fast, 100 jog; 50 fast, 50 jog (total distance: 6.9 kilometers).

Downhill Runs. Developed by running guru Arthur Lydiard, the idea is to run down hills going faster than is possible on the flats. Ideally, the hill should be from 400 to 800 meters long and 80 to 200 meters high. Avoid roads and other hard surfaces unless you wear highly cushioned shoes.

After a proper warm-up, run flat out down the hill, waving your arms in an exaggerated manner. You should feel on the verge of being out of control. At the bottom, jog 200 meters, sprint 200 meters, jog another 200 meters, and then sprint back up the hill.

Repeat three to six times per session, depending on the length and slope of the hill. Don't overdo it the first few times, lest you strain hamstrings or Achilles tendons.

Running Rough Ground

The ability to glide across rough ground is tied to leg strength, mobility, and coordination. You can enhance these skills by running through such terrain and by doing specific exercises that target the relevant skills and muscles.

Running through the woodsy terrain favored by orienteering course setters demands a unique style, a high knee lift that raises the feet above obstacles but does not alter the body's center of gravity. (Watch film of caribou running for some tips.) This must be combined with the balance necessary to cope with unsure footing. Experience will teach you how to hold back weight from a foot until it can "feel" secure footing; meanwhile, the other foot is bearing the weight with a half hop, similar to a skip.

Another way to improve coordination and balance is to run smooth surfaces after dark. When you are unsure of your footing, it forces you to lift your knees and to delay committing your full body weight. Go slow enough to avoid sprained or broken ankles.

The following drills and exercises will place even greater demands on your legs and thus strengthen them.

- Run up hills. This forces the legs to work harder as they must drive your body upward as well as forward. Besides including hills in your LSD, add them to your fartleks and intervals. Take it easy at first—those darn hamstrings—and work up gradually to more and more repetitions.
- Run in sand, mud, tilled land, or marshes. Lacking a firm base against which the feet can push, these types of terrain force you to work harder to lift your legs.
- Even when using a trail for fast navigation, orienteer while running next to it. In training, do off-trail fartleks, alternat-

ing between longer bursts in tough going and shorter, faster bursts in very tough going.

- Do weight training to combat specific muscle weaknesses. Orienteers should focus on gaining strength and suppleness in the feet, ankles, knees, hips, stomach, and back. Lifting weights just a few minutes a day can net impressive results. (Weight training should never be attempted without instruction or supervision.)

- Play other sports. Any strenuous sport will contribute to basic fitness, but some will have greater cross-over benefits for orienteering. A spirited game of soccer, for example, forces competitors to run for sustained periods and to exercise the fake-left-and-go-right muscles and instincts, thereby enhancing skills useful to orienteers. Baseball, bocce ball, and badminton, to name but three, are all less effective in that regard.

Running While Navigating

All training should include mental training, since orienteers must be able to think clearly at race pace. They must be able to make intelligent route choices while breathing hard. This is where fitness training meshes with orienteering technique training, where the physical meets the mental.

The brain requires a continuous supply of oxygen and glucose to function. The athlete who can exercise intensely and continue to feed the brain will be effective.

Your goal should be to improve both fitness and technical skills to the point that neither running nor navigating takes all your energy. Exercises and drills that incorporate map reading and route decisions along with physical workouts can help you improve (see chapter 10).

Even when you're not working out, there are plenty of opportunities to train your mind. For example, note a feature in the distance and estimate its distance from you; check the distance by pacing. You could also imagine what a map of the features around you would look like, contours and all. You can do this walking, standing, or riding. It improves your ability to link contours with real features.

Cool-down

After the aerobic and anaerobic training, you should do a cool-down. No hard workout should end abruptly, lest the blood pool in your extremities. Every session should conclude with five to ten minutes of walking and stretching to enable your body to return to resting levels gradually and efficiently. Repeat the opening stretches and note the greater range of movement that you enjoy now that muscles and tissue are lubricated.

Typical Training Programs

Because people start at different fitness levels and progress at different rates, it's impossible to establish a rigid training program that is right for everyone. Below are sample training weeks for beginning, intermediate, and advanced orienteers. Experiment to find the program or amalgam of programs that works for you.

UNFIT BEGINNER

Monday	20-minute walk/jog
Tuesday	Rest
Wednesday	O-club meeting
Thursday	Rest or other sport
Friday	20-minute walk/jog
Saturday	Rest or other sport
Sunday	Orienteering

Note: Beginners should start with walks interspersed with short jogs and gradually increase the running until they can run 3 or 4 kilometers without stopping.

FAIRLY FIT INTERMEDIATE

Monday	20-minute jog
Tuesday	35-minute run with map
Wednesday	O-club night
Thursday	45-minute run/fartlek
Friday	20-minute run with map
Saturday	15-minute jog or rest
Sunday	Orienteering

Note: Fitness will likely vary from orienteering season to off-season and after layoffs. Adjust your training sessions accordingly.

SUPERFIT ADVANCED

Monday	30-minute steady run (A.M.)
	60-minute steady run (P.M.)
Tuesday	30-minute run with map (A.M.)
	45-minute run in terrain (midday)
	60-minute fartlek/intervals (P.M.)
Wednesday	30-minute steady run (A.M.)
	45-minute fartlek or club training (P.M.)
Thursday	30-minute run with map (A.M.)
	70-minute fartlek/intervals (midday or P.M.)
Friday	30-minute steady run (A.M.)
	45-minute rough terrain (midday)
	50- to 60-minute steady run (P.M.)
Saturday	If competition on Sunday, 20- to 30-minute jog;
	if not, 70-plus-minute fartlek or in terrain
Sunday	Orienteering event or run two hours or more

Note: You have to work up to an ambitious schedule like this, usually over many years. It is the product of dedication and good health.

Strategy

Good judgment comes from experience,
and experience comes from bad judgment.
—Barry LePatner

PRE-RACE PLANNING

Planning for a race is serious business. Even if you don't expect to do well—and it's best to think otherwise—you should adhere to a schedule. Figure out what time you want to be at the starting line and work backward. Budget your time carefully, beginning several days before the competition. A rough schedule might look like this:

1. Be at the start area 10:00 A.M., Saturday, July 10.
2. Leave time before that to walk to the start.
3. Leave time before that to register, relax, visit, review meet materials, and organize punch card, description sheet, compass and map, glasses, and fanny pack.
4. Leave time before that to drive to the meet site.
5. Leave time before that for breakfast. Most competitors don't like to eat closer than two hours before running.
6. Before the day of a meet, your goals might include tapering workout time, sleeping well, prehydration, and adjusting for jet leg and/or travel time.

Preparation Checklist

As you do more events, you will become familiar with organization and procedure. But you should never stop asking and answering the important questions, such as:

- Are the start and registration in the same area? If not, how far is it from registration to start?
- Is the route marked on the map?
- Are toilets available?
- Where can I warm up? Can I leave my warm-up clothing at the start? Will someone take it to the finish?
- Am I dressed properly for the terrain and weather?
- Have I had enough fluids?
- What time is the first start? How many minutes between starts? Do they run on time?
- Are my laces tied and taped?
- Is my compass functioning?
- What does the area near the start look like in terms of terrain and vegetation?
- Is the finish near the start?
- In which direction is the first control? Where are the others on my course going? (If you can see them heading for the first control, which is often the case, then the organizers have not done their job properly.)

Modify and add to your list as you gain experience and hone your preparation strategy. Everyone prepares differently, so borrow the best of other competitors' techniques. On the other hand, don't overwhelm yourself with new information and new skills during preparation, warm-up, and at the start. Use only practiced skills and strategies during an event.

If you suffer from pre-event anxiety, do a longer warm-up. Activity absorbs anxiety.

Time your arrival at the starting area so that you only have five to ten minutes before you are called to the line. You can use the walk/jog/run to the starting area as part of your warm-up. In cold or wet weather, stay as warm and dry as possible. Drink plenty of fluids. Few people drink enough water. You should make it a habit to drink before you become thirsty. High-quality sports drinks, such as ERG, are effective, especially for hot weather and hard runs. Some orienteers carry a water bottle, but there is always water on the longer courses.

Adjusting for Elevation

If you plan to work out or compete at high altitudes, you should understand the physiological effects of thinner air. Most of us live near the bottom of a ten-mile-deep ocean of air. This air, having weight and being compressible, becomes denser as it gets deeper. At sea level, we are adapted to this density, or pressure, which is fifteen pounds per square inch. When we gulp in air, the fifteen pounds of pressure forces sufficient oxygen through the thin linings of our lungs to give our blood what it needs to sustain us.

If you were to orienteer at Lake Tahoe (6,229 feet above sea level) or high on the inhospitable flanks of Mount Washington (6,288 feet), the thinner air would adversely affect your physiological performance. (Many people find running at a high altitude relatively easy at first, but then the symptoms become more severe.) As you climb, the pressure continues to drop. At 10,000 feet, it is down to ten pounds, and much less oxygen is forced through the linings of the lungs. The blood may carry as much as 15 percent less than its normal load of oxygen, a shortage that can cause headaches, fatigue, and shortness of breath. To meet the demands of high-elevation travel, the body restricts blood flow to the organs in favor of the needy muscles. In many people, this disturbs digestion to the point of nausea and weakness. At 18,000 feet, the air pressure is only half what it is at sea level, and almost no one escapes unpleasant symptoms. For most, mental processes are dulled, decision-making suffers, and vision weakens.

The only solution is to acclimatize—that is, to adjust to the new altitude. Live there if possible. Failing that, arrive a few days early for a competition at altitude. A normal, healthy person acclimatized only to sea level will feel the effects of even moderate exercise at 6,000 feet.

Everybody must go through the acclimatization process, no matter how many times they have been to high altitude. There is some evidence that climbers adapt a little better if they have regularly been to high altitudes; nevertheless, even accomplished climbers of Himalayan peaks will be off their game, perhaps severely, if they go from sea level to 12,000 feet without acclimatizing.

Conditioning and downing copious fluids seem to help a little, but the main criterion for successful adaptation to high altitude is what is called the hypoxic drive to breathe. Simplified, it is a measure of how much compensatory breathing you do when your tissues get underoxygenated, as they do at altitude.

ROUTE CHOICE

Well-designed courses (above the White level) try to present more than one route between some of the controls. They should make orienteers think carefully before making their choices.

Straight-line travel in hilly terrain is rarely possible. Nature is forever throwing up obstacles, forcing the orienteer to consider alternatives, some of which can be very difficult. On the other hand, relatively fast corridors may be picked out through careful map reading. Navigation has now become route finding.

When confronting a tough route choice, there's nothing like the knowledge that comes from years of experience solving problems by map. In the meantime, you should consider several variables when calculating how to get quickly from here to there.

One variable is other people. If you are traveling in a group, as you might in the beginning or when doing ROGAINE or Military-O, you should consider the relative strengths of your teammates. Physically, you will only be as strong as your weakest member; keep that in mind when weighing the shorter but more arduous route.

As for technical skills, one teammate may be especially strong with a compass, another with a map. Both talents and shortcomings should be known to the group; give everyone a chance to contribute from his or her unique pool of knowledge. Even if there is only one "expert" on the team, encourage discussion whenever time is not critical. Everyone has a unique perspective, and diverse minds chewing on a problem can yield impressive results. Discussion tends to cast out bad decisions, causing sound ones to emerge. Thus the leader becomes more coordinator than dictator.

For the most part, however, you will travel alone and your dialogue will be an internal one. The questions you will ask yourself over and over are these: "Can I go from here to there in a straight line?" "If not, why not?" "What are my alternatives?"

The answer to that last, crucial question will be based on the following factors:

- Runnability, which is influenced by such variables as footing, wet ground, and undergrowth.
- Physical obstacles, usually in the form of steep slopes, thick vegetation, or bodies of water.
- Land that is out-of-bounds, which may be private property, cultivated land, or worse.
- Technical difficulty, including availability of paths, trails, roads, handrails, catching features, and attack points.
- Personal talents, such as speed on flats, strength on hills, and navigation ability.

Long Easy Way Versus Short Hard Way

This is the most common dilemma for an orienteer. The issue usually boils down to how to assess the relative costs, in time and energy, of two disparate routes—for example, a circuitous but well-trodden path versus a direct but topographically challenging cross-country route. The answer will depend on the relative distances and challenges of the two routes.

One of those challenges is slope or height gain. Climbing a steep hill can quickly take a toll. Relatively fit athletes can run on a horizontal treadmill for hours, but tilt the running platform a mere 15 degrees, and within minutes most are toast.

Learn to distinguish between productive and unproductive climbing. Unproductive climbing means that the height is not retained. If your next control is 25 meters above your present location, then a 25-meter ascent is unavoidable. But if the two controls are nearly the same altitude, going up a 25-meter hill means eventually going down it, thereby crossing a lot of unproductive contours.

The very general rule is that every 15 meters of elevation gain takes about as much time as running 100 meters on level ground. If your map's contour interval is 5 meters, then climbing from one contour line to the next is roughly equivalent to running 30 meters on the level plus the actual distance. You can use this formula to estimate whether it's faster to go over or around a hill.

Referring to figure 18, let's say you're trying to get from here to there. The length of the direct northerly route over the hill is one kilometer with a 180-meter elevation gain. The circuitous southern route is flat and two kilometers long. According to our formula, 180 meters of elevation gain equals almost 1,200 meters added to the 1,000 meters of its length, for a total of 2,200 meters. That is longer than the 2,000-meter (two-kilometer) southern route. The best choice, then, is to go around the hill.

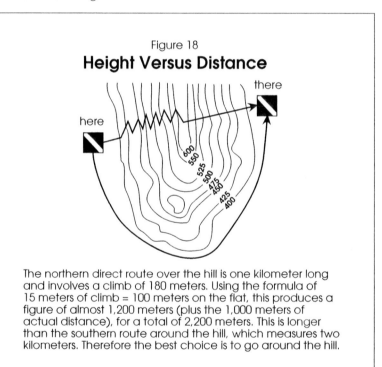

Figure 18
Height Versus Distance

The northern direct route over the hill is one kilometer long and involves a climb of 180 meters. Using the formula of 15 meters of climb = 100 meters on the flat, this produces a figure of almost 1,200 meters (plus the 1,000 meters of actual distance), for a total of 2,200 meters. This is longer than the southern route around the hill, which measures two kilometers. Therefore the best choice is to go around the hill.

Runnability
The above example assumes that the running surfaces of the two routes are similar, but often one of them offers a relatively smooth

trail or road that tips the scales in its favor. Picking your way over huge boulders or through thorny underbrush can deplete you before your time.

Compare route choices in a controlled environment. Select an area with as many of the following features as possible: small hill, large hill, small reentrant, large reentrant. Place streamers on both sides of the hills and both sides of the reentrants. Time yourself running over the hills and around the hills, resting in between. Do the same for the reentrants. Compare the times, and determine whether it is best to run straight or on the contour for each type of terrain.

If you're going to make intelligent route choices, you have to know how fast you are over different terrain. Time yourself over 400 meters and keep track of those times. Your list might look like this:

    a.   Good, flat trail or road—two minutes
    b.   Open uncultivated land—three minutes
    c.   Open forest—four minutes
    d.   Forest with light underbrush—six minutes
    e.   Heavy underbrush—eight minutes

Once you have calculated your times, you need to think in terms of ratios. For example, $4 \times a = e$ tells you that a circuitous path can be four times longer but just as quick as a direct route through heavy underbrush; and $2 \times a = c$ tells you that 400 meters of open forest is comparable in running time to 200 meters of flat trail.

Vegetation

As a stand of trees matures, it chokes out most of the larger vegetation on the forest floor. When conditions prevent the growth of larger species, small brush can thrive. It tends to do well, for example, in stream valleys and in exposed stretches subject to harsh winds and cold temperatures.

Jungles of interwoven vegetation can be miserable for orienteers and should be avoided if at all possible. Identified as the darkest green on an O-map, it is usually referred to in the legend as "Thick underbrush" or simply "Fight," which often translates to "Impassable."

The best forest running (mapped white) is often in a mature forest. Large trees, besides choking off underbrush, tend to lose their lower branches, making running easier. On the other hand, young, closely nestled saplings can be merely slow (light green) or as impenetrable as gorse (dark green).

Many an onrushing orienteer has been slowed by deadfalls. It is one thing to dance around vertical trees, but quite another to skirt horizontal ones. The latter can be time-consuming and exhausting.

STRATEGIC DEVICES AND TECHNIQUES
For maximum success, take what the terrain gives you and the map shows you. Make use of the following strategic devices.

Handrails
Handrails are linear features, such as trails, streams, fences, and power lines, which can guide an orienteer along a route. Beginner's courses rely on obvious handrails, while intermediate and advanced courses tend to use more subtle forms, such as ridges, hillsides, distinct changes in contour spacing, and vegetation boundaries.

In order to reduce the time spent looking at the map, a few orienteers have utilized photographic memories. John Disley tells of Magne Lysfad, a Norwegian forestry worker who won the first European championships in 1962. "He was able to memorize ten square inches of a map at a glance and then run confidently through the terrain ticking off in his head paths, valleys, and streams as he reached them." If you lack such facility, look at the map often.

Handrails can dramatically cut the time spent consulting map and compass. For example, if you know you're going to travel beside a stream for 200 meters before veering off to the next control, you can concentrate on what lies ahead.

Collecting Features (fig 19)

A collecting feature is one that crosses your direction of travel before or after the control. Orienteers use it to funnel or direct themselves en route and to indicate their distance relative to the control. Examples of collecting features include trails, ponds, and streams.

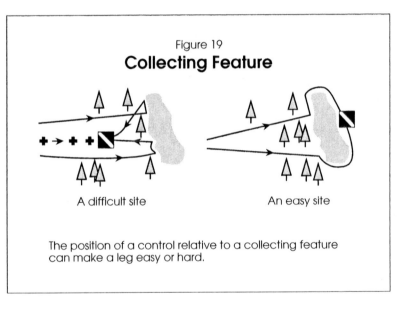

Figure 19
Collecting Feature

A difficult site   An easy site

The position of a control relative to a collecting feature can make a leg easy or hard.

Catching Features (fig 20)

Catching features are linear—roads, fences, ponds, or power lines— and usually perpendicular to your route and past the control. They catch your attention and effectively prevent you from further over- shooting the control. As orienteers near a control, they should become alert to both catching and collecting features, and use them to locate the control or avoid major error.

Improve your ability to use collecting and catching features by practicing in areas with plenty of linear features. Start out navigating legs with conspicuous collecting features (trails, streams, reentrants, large clearings) and catching features (trails, streams, ridges, lake shores). Run quickly to the feature, and then use fine orienteering to reach the control. Discuss route choices.

Figure 20
Catching Feature

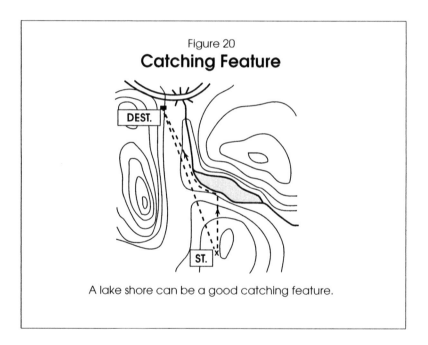

A lake shore can be a good catching feature.

Attack Points

When choosing your route, make sure it includes a definite attack point—a relatively obvious landmark within 50 to 100 meters of the control. Try to use an attack point as close as possible to the control, one that provides the best possible view of the terrain between attack point and control. For example, if the control marker is located on a slope, try to select an attack point above the control.

Once you find the attack point, you can switch to fine orienteering over a small area in order to zero in on the control. Because most courses are designed around attack points, it's helpful to try to figure out which ones the course maker had in mind.

Beginners on the White course don't need to find an attack point because control markers are hung on obvious features, and the routes between controls usually follow linear features, such as trails or streams.

Beginners on the Yellow course use distinct trails and junctions, bends, and field corners as attack points.

Intermediate competitors may also use trail junctions, trail bends, and field corners as attack points. More often, though, they rely on terrain features such as hills, reentrants, and marshes.

Advanced orienteers tend to take more direct routes through the terrain, using smaller, less distinct attack points that an intermediate might miss.

Attack from above. When controls are located on slopes, try to approach from above. Do your climbing early. This gives you the widest field of vision, enough perhaps to see another orienteer or to pick out your route to the following control.

When you descend to a control, you are also fresher than if you had just climbed up to it. This better enables you to handle the challenges of fine orienteering.

NAVIGATION
Rough and Fine Orienteering (fig 21)
Rough orienteering is the technique of looking at the map to glean a general idea of the direction and distance to the next control, then running to a collecting feature. The rough orienteer navigates by large terrain features, such as swamps, ponds, fields, and reentrants.

As you near the control, you should switch to fine orienteering, a slower, less efficient, but more precise method of navigation. With fine orienteering, smaller features are used to check and recheck your position on the map.

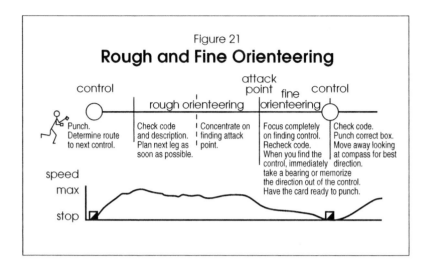

Figure 21
Rough and Fine Orienteering

Aiming Off (fig 22)

This technique, used in conjunction with a collecting or catching feature, is the deliberate selection of a route that aims a few degrees off target to one side or the other. In this way, when you reach the collecting feature, you know which way to turn to find the control.

If you seem to have trouble with this technique, you may be exaggerating your aim. Don't go too far astray from your desired route—50 to 200 meters to one side or the other should be plenty.

Practice aiming off from the comfort of your own home. Select a map with many linear features, and then pick imaginary controls near those features. Draw a line showing how you would aim off and intersect the linear feature, then another to show how you would approach the control. When finished, discuss route choices with your mentors.

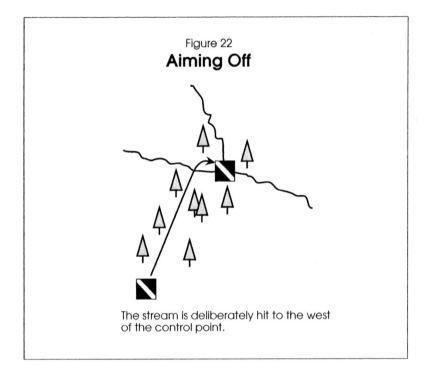

Figure 22
Aiming Off

The stream is deliberately hit to the west of the control point.

Contouring

Contouring is the art of moving along a slope while remaining at the same elevation—that is, on the same contour. First you have to identify when to use it, and then you have to be able to traverse a hillside without climbing or descending. It's harder than you may think.

The lower your level of fitness, the greater the importance of running around difficult landforms. Advanced orienteers may be able to sustain a climb without losing time or energy, but even super-fit competitors will sometimes benefit from the technique of contouring.

Planning

Always plan where you want to go ahead of time, even if it's only nanoseconds ahead of time. Moving before you have a sense of where you are supposed to go is bound to cause errors. This is an easy trap to fall into for serious competitors because of the constant

To improve your ability to visualize contours, practice with a group in an area with small and medium-size reentrants. Pick a contour and have one orienteer walk away from the group while remaining on the same contour. The remaining group members can help by telling him when he is going up or down. The leader says "Stop" when the walker has covered about 10 or 15 meters; another walker then goes 10 to 15 meters beyond the first. Continue until each member of the group has become part of a human contour line.

pressure not to lose time. Follow your plan, unless the terrain makes it inappropriate, at which point you should select a new plan.

Relocation

Let's say that despite all your planning and all those strategic aids, you get lost. It happens to the best. Maybe the biggest difference between an elite and an average orienteer is how each copes with being lost, how well each relocates.

If you get lost, you must stop and collect your thoughts. You hope the collection goes swiftly, but do whatever it takes, because running around aimlessly is exhausting and counterproductive. Orient your map. Try to correlate the features you see with the features on the map. Calculate where you might have gone from your last known position. If you still can't figure your position, use your compass and head for the nearest line feature. Try to locate your position on that.

When you have failed to find a control from a good attack point, it might behoove you to circle the area where the control should be. However, if you have not been careful from the attack point or if visibility is poor, it is safest to return to the attack point and try again—at a walking pace.

In trying to estimate distance covered, keep in mind that you will probably not have gone as far as you think you have.

DEALING WITH COURSE DESIGN

Course setters have a difficult job. They must establish several fair, reasonable courses with varying degrees of difficulty. They endeavor to please both experienced orienteers, who demand fairly wild terrain in order to test their limits, and novices, who require a tamer landscape.

The more you can get into the mind of a course setter, the more successful you will be at finding controls. In other words, understanding a little about course design can make you a better navigator. Course setters generally rely on these guidelines:

- The actual control marker should be very visible on beginning courses, exactly at or on the designated feature.
- Markers should not be hung in such dense undergrowth that they are obscured when you are at the control.
- Early legs of the course should not pass near later controls, lest late starters in the early stages of a race gain unfair knowledge regarding the position of later controls, or be tempted to punch out of order.
- There should be no "dog-leg" angles at the controls (fig 23). This is to ensure that the natural exit from a control site does not overlap the likely entry route. In this way, designers prevent competitors from being directed to a control by departing runners.
- Similarly, controls should not be selected so that the probable route taken by departing runners inadvertently "catches" and assists lost runners (fig 24).
- For intermediate and advanced competitors, there should be, if possible, a choice of routes offered between one control and the next, even if the choice is between two comparable routes. This is particularly important if the course is

Figure 23
Arrangement of Control Positions to Avoid Dog-Legs in the Course

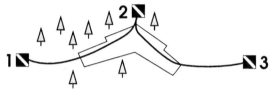

Poor site for control 3 as it produces a dog-leg.

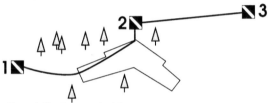

Good site for control 3.

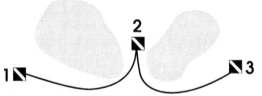

Poor site for control 3 as it produces a dog-leg.

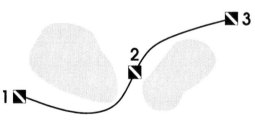

Good site for control 3.

Figure 24

Leaving a Control

The probable route taken away from a control should not "catch" runners.

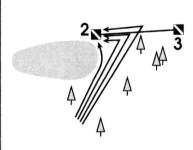
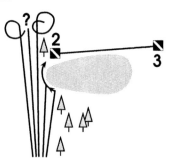

Poor—outgoing runners "catch" and direct lost incoming runners to the control.

Good—lost runners are not helped by outgoing runners.

Figure 25

Unfair Choice

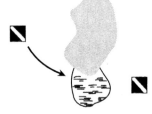

An unindicated marsh at the south end of the lake makes the choice of routes around the lake unfair.

By changing the position of the second control, luck is taken out of the choice. Everyone will get involved with the marsh and the subsequent detour.

technically easy. Care should be taken to assure that sheer luck does not determine the outcome. For example, in figure 25, a marsh at the south end of the lake could mean problems for the orienteer who chooses that route. By changing the position of the next control, luck is eliminated, and everyone will have to tangle with the marsh.

- There should not be a control positioned in such a way as to encourage the competitor to traverse dangerous terrain or areas that are out-of-bounds, such as private property. Given the position of the second control in figure 26, the logical route is to the east of the lake, but that encourages the orienteer to traverse a potentially dangerous cliff. We see a preferable alternative in figure 26, as the second control is now positioned to encourage a safer westerly route.

- Controls should be selected to encourage a variety of navigation problems and physical effort.

- Controls on novice courses are generally set at spots that target at least one obvious man-made feature, such as a trail junction, fence, or bridge over a river. Advanced courses tend to emphasize strictly natural features, such as knolls, cliffs, and small contour features.

- In advanced courses, controls should be selected so that the accurate navigator receives due reward. One way of accomplishing this is to place the control a couple of hundred meters on the near side of a collecting feature. In this way, the casual orienteer will, if he is off course, have to retrace his steps from the collecting feature, while the accomplished navigator is more apt to hit the target on the first try.

- There should be a clearing, an unobstructed run of 200 meters or so, between the last control and the finish. This allows spectators to see the last part of the race.

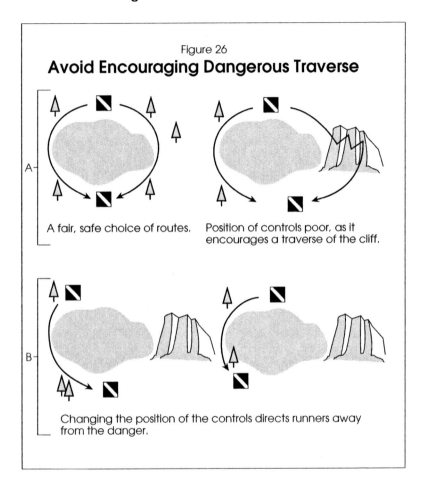

Figure 26
Avoid Encouraging Dangerous Traverse

A fair, safe choice of routes.

Position of controls poor, as it encourages a traverse of the cliff.

Changing the position of the controls directs runners away from the danger.

ORIENTEERING SEASONS

Different seasons mean different orienteering conditions, which in turn demand adjustments by the orienteer. In the spring, you should expect waterways to be full. At times, streams become rivers and marshes become ponds. In the summer in California, streams and ponds are often dry, but this is less predictable in the eastern United States.

With seasonal changes, the foliage ranges from nonexistent to thick. Thus, visibility varies widely, with a dramatic effect on technical difficulty and runnability. Areas that are overgrown in the summer may be very runnable in fall and early spring.

Equipment

Nature uses as little as possible of anything.
—*Johannes Kepler*

Orienteers need little equipment and are allowed to dress any way they like. Nevertheless, the right gear and clothing can make life in the woods, or on the practice field, a whole lot easier.

CLOTHES
Training Shoes
If you're going to work out, you will need a good pair of running shoes. A billion or so people in the world wear no shoes at all, and on average they have fewer foot problems than we do. One reason: shoes that don't fit. You need to shop carefully when making such an important purchase.

If you have an old pair of running or walking shoes, take them with you when you look for a new pair; a knowledgeable salesperson can evaluate your form, and hence your needs, by looking at the wear pattern on your old shoes. Remember to take along socks. Don't be afraid to jog or power-walk around the store in the new shoes. What's a few minutes of looking geeky compared to getting the right shoes?

Get the right fit. All size-10s are not alike. There should be one-half inch of space between your longest toe and the tip of the shoe when you put all your weight on that foot.

Compare the left and right shoes. Make sure they are the same length and width. Put the shoes side by side on a flat surface and look at them from behind. The uppers should be perpendicular to the soles; they should not lean to one side.

Test how the shoe moves. Hold on to the front and back of the shoe and bend it. It should bend just where your foot bends—at the ball. If the shoe bends at the midfoot, it will offer little support. It should bend neither too easily nor too stiffly, though walking shoes are more rigid than running shoes. Hold the heel and try to move the rigid section at the back of the shoe; it shouldn't move from side to side.

If you overpronate—your foot rolls in significantly—look for a shoe with a good arch support, a straight (rather than curved) last, and a less flexible sole, especially along the inside edge. If you supinate—your foot rolls outward significantly—look for a shoe with a strong heel counter, a substantial yet somewhat soft midsole, a curved last, and a flexible sole.

No matter how sweet those new running shoes feel in the store, break them in before you take them out for a long run. Purchase new shoes before old ones completely die, and wear the new ones on short workouts every two or three days. By the time the old shoes are completely gone, the new ones will be comfortable.

A friend of mine finds athletic shoes to be hard on his Achilles tendons. Accordingly, he slits his shoes about an inch down the back, effectively relieving the pressure on the Achilles without shortening the life of the shoe.

Speaking of shoe life, tests have shown that virtually all running shoes lose about a third of their cushioning after 500 miles of use. This typically happens before the outer sole or upper shows wear.

Orienteering Shoes

Many serious orienteers wear shoes made specifically for their sport. Good orienteering shoes offer rubber studs or metal spikes for good traction; strong construction and good support to withstand the punishment of moving through rough terrain; waterproof and/or quick-drying tops; lighter weight than most running shoes.

Orienteering shoes range from Botas, a $45 shoe from Czechoslovakia, to the Silva "Super Grip" from Sweden, at $132. A substitute that will satisfy all but the elite competitors is a good pair of rubber-studded softball or rugby shoes.

Stockings
Experienced orienteers will dress their legs for bush-whacking.

Bramble Bashers. Made in Scandinavia, the birthplace of orienteering, these special socks have a smooth plastic finish on the front to shed brush and thorns.

Gaiters. Gaiters wrap around the ankle and shin to protect that vulnerable opening between socks and pants. Orienteering gaiters have pretty much replaced bramble bashers for the modern orienteer. Generally lightweight, some have a padded front to protect the shins and stirrups instead of lace ties. For sizing, measure shin length from the bottom of the kneecap to the front bend of the ankle.

Shorts
Nylon shorts, slit up the side, are light, cool, and dry quickly. In weather that's chilly but not cold enough for long pants, cotton shorts add a touch of warmth. Nylon or Lycra tights beneath shorts add more warmth and some protection. Orienteers eschew shorts in the worst areas because of the need to protect their legs from undergrowth.

Headgear
Some see a hat as optional equipment, but when the weather gets extreme, some kind of headgear can be important. At least 40 percent of lost body heat escapes through the head, and hats keep in much of that heat. Consider a stocking cap in the extreme cold. Even if you choose to orienteer with a bare head, you may want the warmth of a hat before and after the event. When it's hot, a golf visor will shade your eyes and slow the rivulets of sweat streaming down your brow. Thin-haired orienteers should protect the tops of their heads from sun exposure with some kind of hat or sunscreen.

Orienteering Suits
Most serious orienteers dress in durable, breathable nylon suits

(complete suit: top with pants or knickers), especially designed for running and orienteering. Sizes are unisex; designs and colors vary. Note that most large clubs have uniforms, O-suits in club colors.

MAPS

When you sign in at an orienteering meet, you will receive a map for that day's course. Before then, however, you should acquire and gain familiarity with topographical maps, of which orienteering maps are one very detailed version.

Although U.S. Geological Survey (USGS) maps are not used in orienteering, they are useful for mastering the art of reading topo maps. You may have to go no farther than your local outdoor store to find the USGS topographic maps you need. If you need maps of obscure areas or other states (including Bureau of Land Management holdings), direct your inquiries to the USGS National Cartographic Information Center, 507 National Center, Reston, VA 22092. Once you have identified the specific maps you need, you can order individual topos by mail from the USGS.

For areas east of the Mississippi River, including Minnesota, Puerto Rico, and the Virgin Islands, write to the Branch of Distribution, U.S. Geological Survey, 1200 South Eads St., Arlington, VA 22202.

For areas west of the Mississippi River, including Alaska, Hawaii, Louisiana, Guam, and American Samoa, write to the Branch of Distribution, U.S. Geological Survey, Box 25286, Federal Center, Denver, CO 80225.

Ask the USGS to send you a free state index, which identifies the topo maps by name on a grid of the state. The index also lists any special topos, such as for national parks. You can also order a pamphlet that explains the symbols that are common to all topos but are left off the legends of individual maps.

The U.S. Forest Service (USFS) also uses a topographic format for its wilderness maps. Keep in mind that USFS maps are usually copies of USGS originals. As such, they may be plagued by the inevitable maladies of reproduction: misalignment, blurred trails, and free-hand additions. As you improve your map-reading skills, you will learn to recognize potentially misleading information.

For maps of national forests, write to the U.S. Forest Service Information Office, Room 3238, P.O. Box 2417, Washington, DC 20013.

COMPASS

Hand compasses range in price and quality from the prize in a box of Cracker Jacks to the Brunton pocket transit, with digital readout, field case, battery charger, and tripod (over $1,000). If you intend to use your compass with topographic maps, you will need an orienteering compass, complete with protractor baseplate and revolving housing. The Silva compass has dominated the market for so long that its name is practically generic. The company makes at least eighteen compass models, including one for the blind and another for Muslims with a second needle always pointing toward Mecca.

The important qualities when shopping for a compass:

- Versatility—it must do bearings.
- Speed—how fast does it dampen oscillation?
- Durability—is it tough? Cliff Jacobson says he once had a jeep run over a Silva Ranger and, although the cover was smashed, it worked fine.
- Amenities—the little things. Do the scales on the baseplate conform to the ones on your maps? Is there a built-in magnifying glass for reading detail and the fine print?
- Accessories—does it adjust to different map scales? Additional scales can be purchased separately. Silva makes a pace counter that can be attached to the baseplate. This is a simple clicker that allows you to keep track of paces by flicking it with your thumb as you run.

The good news is that the price of a Silva—or its main competitors, Suunto and Moscow—is still closer to the Cracker Jacks version than to the expensive Brunton. As of this writing, a Silva Starter, good for young children, is $10, and the Silva Type 5 Jet is about $70. The Type 5 Jet has a powerful magnet attached to a leveling plate that provides super-quick needle dampening and superior stability when you're running rough terrain. Incidentally, the Silva Type 5 and Type 6 Jet compasses were used by thirty of the thirty-six medal winners in the 1993 World Orienteering Championships. A good and basic model that will get most people going is the Silva Polaris.

A compass needle will continue to oscillate for some time unless it is damped, either by light-viscosity oil (liquid damping) or by magnetism (induction damping). Liquid-damped needles stop moving in about three seconds; induction-damped needles take much longer. They are also heavier, bulkier, and more expensive. The result is that almost all the best hand compasses are liquid-filled.

Thumb Compass. Many advanced orienteers have switched to a thumb compass. This is a highly specialized O-compass that the fastest competitors like because it doesn't require slowing down to take a bearing—the map is always set with the compass. The runner keeps the compass on the oriented and folded map as he runs, with the needle aligned with the magnetic north lines and the edge of the compass aligned with the leg he is on. The compass is strapped to his thumb.

ACCESSORIES
Magnifying Lens
If you are farsighted, you will need magnification to help you read the map. You can carry a small lens or use the one on most orienteering compasses, but some people find it more convenient to wear headsets with magnifying lenses that flip down for reading and up

for running. You can obtain this headgear from orienteering vendors or where dental equipment is sold.

Joe Scarborough makes a magnifier designed for a thumb compass (but which can also be attached to a baseplate). It allows the magnifier to remain on the map for reading on the run. According to Joe, "It is very good for the over-forty speed demon."

Map Case
Clear plastic map cases keep maps clean and dry, and they are supple enough to fold. They are generally provided at meets but can also be found at sporting goods and stationary stores. Large ziplock bags also work quite well. You can carry your control card and description sheet in the map case.

Repellent
Mosquitoes and flies are into nature—in a big way. Ticks can also be a big problem in some areas. Using repellent to ward off the little devils may make the difference between a fine time in the woods and abject misery. Look for half-ounce plastic bottles with a moderate amount of DEET (diethyl metatoluamide). (See chapter 5 for details.)

A lotion such as Tecnu is valuable in areas with poison oak or ivy. Some people are very sensitive to such poisonous plants.

Frivolities
There are a whole host of T-shirts, sweatshirts, caps, and jackets decorated with a variety of logos, maps, sayings ("Give me a map and I'm magic"), and cartoon characters. You also can buy bumper stickers ("Orienteers Find a Way"; "Orienteering—Cunning Running"), decals, posters, stationery, mugs, tote bags, headbands, jigsaw puzzles, books, videos, and ornaments. They won't make you run faster or navigate better, but they're fun.

ORGANIZERS' GEAR
Plan to hold your own orienteering meet? You may need any or all of the following: control markers, punches, cards, directional signs, map and/or compass cases, record-keeping materials,

organizing manual, and, of course, nonmagnetic staples that won't affect compasses.

Consider the following USOF-approved vendors for orienteering shoes, clothing, equipment, and accessories:

A&E Enterprises
Al and Edie Smith
74 Decorah Dr.
St. Louis, MO 63146
314-872-3165

J. Berman's Orienteering Supply
253 Amherst Rd. #2B
Sunderland, MA 01375
413-665-7822

Orienteer California
Bruce Wolfe
46 Craig Ave.
Piedmont, CA 94611

Orienteering Services USA
Bill Wildprett
P.O. Box 1604
Binghamton, NY 13902

Selected Rules of Orienteering

Rules governing orienteering events in the United States are maintained by the United States Orienteering Federation (USOF). All meets in the United States are hosted by orienteering clubs and classified as "A," "B," or "C." "A" meets are formal, nationally sanctioned events; "B" meets are regional events; "C" meets are considered local events. Meets that have been sanctioned by the USOF must adhere to published rules governing "A" and "B" events. "C" meets are not required to follow USOF rules.

The official USOF rule book is long and technical, and many of the points are of interest only to meet organizers. What follows are the rules that are important to most competitors.

1.1   Competitions described as United States Orienteering Federation (USOF) events and other orienteering events held in conjunction with USOF events shall be organized in accordance with these rules.

2.1   Orienteering is a sport in which the competitor, independently aided by map and compass, must visit in the prescribed order a number of features marked on the map and in the terrain by control flags. In a regular orienteering competition, the task is to run the course in the shortest possible time.

2.2   In orienteering, both the running and navigating skills of the competitor shall be tested, but in such a way that the navigating skill is decisive.

2.3   Orienteering competitions shall be held primarily in forested terrain, which, ideally, is unfamiliar to the competitors.

4.1.1   Competitors are divided into classes based on gender and age as of December 31 of the current year. Eligibility for classes occurs at the beginning of the calendar year in which the competitor reaches a new age group.

4.1.4   No competitor shall be entered in more than one class at a time.

4.1.4.1 Competitors may participate on a noncompetitive course after finishing their competitive course.

4.1.5   In an individual event, groups shall be permitted only in non-competitive categories.

5.5.1   Persons with prior knowledge of the competition area, which they or the meet organizers believe will give them an unfair advantage, are not eligible to compete for awards, titles, or national rankings (see section 35.5).

17.5   When in response to a protest, the Jury determines that any of the following conditions have existed for a substantial group of competitors in a class, then the class or course shall be voided.

a. A control flag is missing.

b. A control flag, the start, or the finish is not within the marked circle or triangle.

c. A control flag is on the wrong feature.

d. The code at the control is different from that on the control description sheet.

19.1   All those involved with the organizing of the event shall maintain the strictest secrecy regarding aspects of the venue, terrain, and courses that are not officially publicized.

24.4   The approximate winning times and lengths of the various courses are as follows:

Course Length	Optimum Winner's Time	Approx. Course
White	30 minutes	3 km or less
Yellow	40 minutes	3.5–4.5 km
Orange	50 minutes	4–5 km
Brown	50 minutes	3.5–4.5 km
Green	50 minutes	4–5 km
Red	60 minutes	5–7 km
Blue	60–80 minutes	7–12 km

24.5   Long O (long-distance orienteering) for which the times and distances of the brown, green, red, and blue courses are increased (by about 50 percent) may be organized. Long O is characterized by long legs with complex route choice problems.

25.1   The competition map shall be marked as follows:

a. The start or map-issue point by an equilateral triangle 7mm per side.

b. The control features by circles 5–6mm in diameter.

c. The finish by two concentric circles 5 and 7mm in diameter.

d. Marked routes by dashed lines.

25.2   The center of any triangle or circle indicates the precise position of the feature, but it shall not be actually marked.

25.3   The control circles shall be numbered showing the required sequence. The numerals shall be printed with their tops oriented exactly toward North. The numbers shall be placed in such a way that they do not conceal important map features.

27.1   The control description serves to clarify the picture of the control site as it appears on the map. It shall describe the control site accurately, but as briefly as possible.

27.2   The control descriptions shall correspond to the "Control Descriptions" of the IOF on all but the White and Yellow courses.

27.2.1   On the White and Yellow courses, English words approximating the meanings and order of the IOF symbols shall be used. When possible, they should be adjacent to the IOF symbols.

28.2   Danger areas shall be marked with both blue and yellow ribbons. When those colors are not possible, others may be substituted if the change is included in the event information.

29.1   Every control feature shall be marked by a control flag.

29.2   The control flag consists of three squares arranged in triangular form. Each square is 30cm x 30cm and is divided diagonally, with one half white and the other half orange.

29.3   The control flag shall be hung at the feature indicated on the map. The position shall be in accordance with the control description.

29.4   The control flag shall be visible by the competitor upon reaching the feature.

29.5   Ideally, control flags shall be situated so that the presence or absence of competitors does not make them easier or harder to locate.

29.6   The relative arrangement of the control flag, control code, and marking devices shall be the same for all control sites on a course.

29.7   Each control location shall be identified by a number (not less than 31), or by up to two letters, which will constitute the control code. The same code shall be included on the control description sheet. The figures shall be black, approximately 6–10cm high with a line width of approximately 6–10mm. Ideally, competitors will be able to read the codes only when immediately at the control flag.

30.2   Using the marking equipment provided at each control site, competitors shall mark the correct box of their control card. They must hand in their control card at the finish. When competitors mark an incorrect box, they should continue the correct sequence beginning with the next box. Disqualifications will be decided by the Jury.

30.4 If a competitor loses a control card, or a control mark is missing, or it is established that the control sites were not visited in the prescribed order, the competitor shall be disqualified, unless an alternate proof is offered and accepted by the Jury.

33.6 All competitors shall have the same amount of time to complete their courses. Unless a longer time is declared in the meet information, the competition time shall be three hours for all events except Long O. Without exception, the time limit for Long O shall be five hours.

33.7 Competitors completing a course in a time greater than the competition time will be designated overtime (OVT) and will not receive a time or place.

33.8 All competitors, whether finished or not, shall report to the finish by the announced closing time of the finish.

35.2 It is forbidden to obtain outside help or collaborate in running or navigating, except in a noncompetitive class.

35.3 A competitor shall not seek to obtain unfair advantage over fellow competitors, nor intentionally run with or behind other competitors in order to profit from their skill.

35.4 Prior investigation of the competition area is forbidden.

35.5 Event organizers are obliged to bar entrants from competing (but not from participating) when they are so well acquainted with the terrain that they would derive substantial advantage over others. In doubtful cases, the matter is decided by the Jury.

36.3 During the competition, only a compass and the map provided by the organizer may be used for navigation.

36.3.1 Personal aids not used directly for navigation are permitted (e.g., magnifying glass, flashlight, cane, eyeglasses).

36.4 The use of any navigation aid other than a compass is prohibited (e.g., transport, electronic apparatus, radio, pedometer, altimeter).

37.2 Competitors shall move in the terrain as silently as possible, and neither by shouting nor by sign give help or do harm to other competitors, nor intentionally draw their attention.

37.3   It is the duty of each competitor to help anyone who is injured.

37.6   Once competitors cross the finish line, their competition is over, and they shall not return to the competition area without permission from the organizer.

37.7   Competitors who do not finish (DNF) must report to the finish and return their control card and map. They shall in no way attempt to influence the competition or other competitors.

38.1   It is forbidden to cause damage to the competition terrain. The competitors are solely responsible for their damage.

38.2   Competitors shall not enter the following areas except when specific permission is included in the event information:
a. Yards and gardens;
b. Sown land or crop land;
c. Limited-access highways or fenced railways;
d. Areas marked "out of bounds."

38.3   In consideration of nature conservation, land owners, and others, barriers and gates opened by competitors shall be closed by same.

If you have questions about these rules or wish to obtain the complete set of rules, contact the USOF Rules Committee.

Rules Committee Chairperson
Joseph Huberman
904 Dorothea Dr.
Raleigh, NC 27603
919-828-6068

Special thanks to Joe Scarborough for his summary.

Games and Exercises

MAP READING

1. Map Orientation

Goal: To learn to orient the map to north and to reorient it as one changes direction

Means: Lining up a map with a sign marked "North"

Activity Level: Standing/walking

Location: Indoor/outdoor

Time Required: Five to ten minutes

Materials: "North" sign, red marker, one map per person

Preparation: Post "North" sign on a wall or on the ground in the proper direction. Mark the north end of each map with a red line.

Start: Participants stand facing the same direction, one arm's length apart, maps on the ground in front of them. Face north, then east, then south, then west, then north again. Note that you moved in relation to the land around you; the land did not move.

Now pick up the map and orient it; that is, point the red edge of the map at the north sign. Note that the map moved in relation to the land. Wander around the area, holding the map about waist level, keeping it oriented as you turn. Instructors should look for problems and assist when necessary.

Variations: (1) Try it in the woods. (2) Use the needle on the compass to stay oriented to north.

2. Room-O

Goal: To learn to relate to a two-dimensional map of a three-dimensional space

Means: Walking a course, finding coded stickers, and unscrambling the code

Activity Level: Walk

Location: Indoor

Time Required: Ten minutes

Materials: Posterboard, marker, seven to ten small stickers, paper and pencil

Preparation: Draw a map of the room. Draw a letter on each sticker (to spell a word when all stickers have been found) and place the stickers on mapped features in the room.

Start: The object is to look at the circles on the map and find the corresponding feature in the room. Write down the letter on each sticker you find. When all the stickers have been found, unscramble the letters to make a word. Begin on "Go."

Periodically rotate the map so that participants must mentally reorient it when they return to review it between sticker searches.

3. Map Symbol Relay

Goal: To learn the international orienteering map symbols

Means: A relay game

Activity Level: Walk/run

Location: Indoor/outdoor

Time Required: Five minutes

Materials: Index cards (5 x 7 inches) with a map legend symbol drawn on one side and a written description of a different symbol on the other side. Provide one set of ten cards for five people. Color-coded cards will keep sets separate.

Preparation: Make cards as shown below. Mark a starting line for the teams. Cluster a set of cards, symbol side up, an exact distance (10, 20, 30 meters) from the start. Leave at least 3 meters between each team's cards (fig 27).

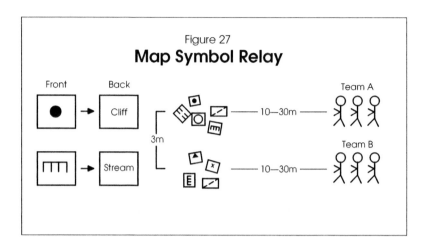

Figure 27
Map Symbol Relay

Start: The group is divided into at least two teams, each with an equal number of players. At "Go," the lead on each team runs from the starting line to her cluster of cards and chooses one card. She races back to her teammates and hands her card to the next person in line, who flips it over and reads the description of a different symbol that she must now find.

Now that player races to the cards and returns with the correct one. The process is repeated until all the team's cards have been retrieved. The first team to collect all its cards wins.

Variations: (1) Teams may be approximately the same ability level, or they may be arranged by course color, with the more advanced teams having farther to run to reach their cards. (2) Use the cards as flash cards for a seated audience.

4. Never a Dull Moment

Goal: To increase the ability to quickly read and remember map detail

Means: Map study
Activity Level: Seated/walk/run
Location: Almost anywhere
Time Required: Varies

Materials: Map or maps

Preparation: Place maps in strategic locations at home and at the office, where they can be studied during free moments.

Start: Place thumb on map and study the area above thumb for one to three seconds. Ask yourself what you saw, especially color and symbols, relationship to other features, orientation, and slope characteristics. Look again to check your accuracy and to note additional features. Repeat until the area is completely described.

Variations: (1) Do while walking, running, waiting in line, or sitting in the doctor's office. (2) If you don't want to carry a map when you run, exercise your memory with license plates, streets, and addresses.

5. Map Memory Relay

Goal: To memorize map and course detail during physical activity

Means: Relay game

Activity Level: Run

Location: Indoor/outdoor

Time Required: Ten to fifteen minutes.

Materials: Two maps for each team, red or purple pens, circle template

Preparation: On each map mark a course with a specific degree of difficulty. Place marked maps at one end of the yard or room; at the other end, place unmarked maps, pens, and circle templates. If outside, you may need map boards.

Start: Divide the group into teams of equal number, each with an unmarked map, pen, and template. On "Go," the lead for each team runs to the map and memorizes the location of the start triangle and as many controls as possible. She then returns to the unmarked map and draws as much of the course as she can recall, including numbered controls and connecting lines. The winner is the first team to finish with all controls correctly drawn and labeled. If no one is perfect, award five points for each correct control, with one point subtracted (up to five) for each millimeter the circle is off.

Variation: If you draw a different course on each map, the teams can swap maps to make new games.

6. Matching Map Pieces Relay

Goal: To enhance map-reading ability by recognition of map detail and orientation of features

Means: Relay game

Activity Level: Seated/walk/run

Location: Indoor/outdoor

Time Required: Varies

Materials: One map puzzle for each team

Preparation: Draw squares on each map, none adjacent to the others. Squares should measure $1^1/2$ x $1^1/2$ inches for beginners and intermediates, 1 x 1 inch for advanced orienteers. Cut out the squares for each map, keep them separate, and put them at one end of the relay area with the teams. At the other end put the map, which now resembles a piece of Swiss cheese. Glue the map and the squares to separate pieces of cardboard to increase durability.

Start: On "Go," the first member of each team selects a square and runs to the cut-out map, where he tries to find the correct square hole in which to insert his piece, properly oriented. He then races back to his team and tags a teammate, who repeats the process. First team to complete its map wins.

Variation: Do this activity seated, with one to three members for each map.

7. Map Walk for Handrails

Goal: To learn to identify handrails on maps and in terrain

Means: A walk with an intermediate or advanced orienteer

Activity Level: Walk

Location: Outdoor

Time Required: Forty-five to sixty minutes

Materials: One map for each person

Preparation: Select an area for a walk that is rich in handrails, which can be followed one to the next. Select handrails appropriate for the group's skill level.

Start: Walk with beginning orienteers, explaining as you go the many faces of handrails (for example, trails, streams, forest boundaries). Stop at times to discuss upcoming handrails. As you see improvement, advance to more subtle features.

8. Jigsaw Map Puzzle (fig 28)

Goal: To enhance the ability to read maps and make associations among map features

Means: Putting together a map puzzle

Activity Level: Seated

Location: Indoor/outdoor

Time Required: Ten to fifteen minutes

Materials: One map for each team or group, prepared as jigsaw puzzles

Preparation: Select a map with plenty of linear features. Glue map to cardboard. Cut the interior of the map into several irregularly shaped pieces, leaving a map border. For a more durable map frame, glue the remaining border to a second piece of cardboard.

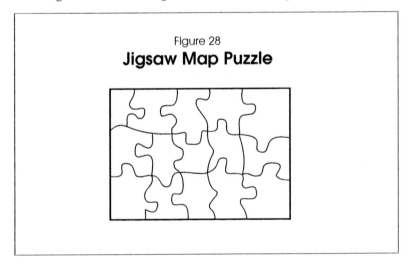

Figure 28
Jigsaw Map Puzzle

Start: Provide each team of three or four orienteers with a map frame and its pieces. The pieces are laid out randomly. On "Go," each group begins to assemble its jigsaw puzzle. Record the time for each group to complete its puzzle. Switch puzzles until all groups have worked all puzzles. Lowest cumulative time wins.

Variations: (1) Set it up as a relay race, with puzzle frames at one end and pieces at the other. (2) Make it harder by cutting the pieces into similar squares.

9. Corridor-O (fig 29)

Goal: To enhance the skills of reading fine map detail and recognizing such detail in the field

Means: Navigation using maps having only corridors between controls

Activity Level: Walk/run

Location: Outdoor

Time Required: Thirty to sixty minutes

Materials: Maps prepared with only corridors visible between controls; additional copies of the map in envelopes, one for each person; and controls

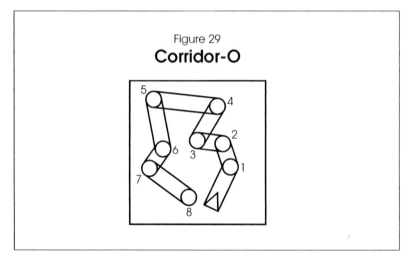

Figure 29
Corridor-O

Preparation: Mark a course on the map, taking care to avoid dangerous or impossible terrain, such as uncrossable streams. Cover the map with tracing paper and mark the course with a corridor between controls that is from 6 to 10 millimeters wide. Number the controls on the paper. Cut out the corridors. Place the paper over the map and photocopy one map for each person. Set the controls.

Start: Provide each orienteer with one corridor map and one complete map to refer to only if lost. Stagger the start. Orienteers navigate using only the information visible in the corridors.

Variations: (1) Send orienteers in pairs. (2) Use a wider corridor for easier orienteering, narrower for harder. (3) Place the complete map in a sealed envelope. The envelope must be sealed at the end to win.

10. Window-O (fig 30)
Goal: To learn to move quickly along a compass bearing for a given distance and to be able to relate terrain features to a map

Means: Navigation using maps having only squares around each control

Activity Level: Walk/run

Location: Outdoor

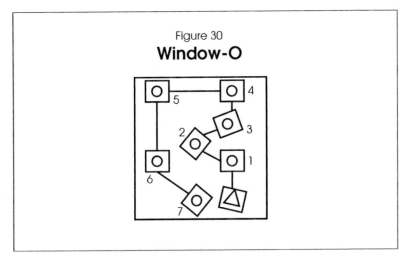

Figure 30
Window-O

Time Required: Thirty to sixty minutes

Materials: One prepared window map, one regular map, and one envelope for each person; controls

Preparation: Mark a course on a map with legs no longer than 400 meters, taking care to avoid difficult or impossible terrain, such as precipitous cliffs or uncrossable marshes. Place tracing paper over the map, and draw a square (1.5 x 1.5 centimeters) around each control. Connect consecutive squares with a line and number the controls on the paper. Cut out the squares. Place the paper over the squares and photocopy one map with windows for each person. Set the controls.

Start: Provide each orienteer with a window map and a complete map sealed in an envelope (to be used only when lost). Orienteers should use their compasses to take a bearing; measure the distance to the next control. While following the bearing and using pacing to estimate distance, study the map within the windows to recognize the area when you reach it. Once within a window, use fine orienteering to locate the control.

Variation: Make larger windows and shorter legs for easier orienteering.

11. Line-O (fig 31)

Goal: To increase the ability to read fine detail on a map and in the field

Means: Navigation using a map with a course indicated by a line

Activity Level: Walk/run

Location: Outdoor

Time Required: Thirty to sixty minutes

Materials: One marked map and pencil per person, controls or streamers

Preparation: On the map mark a 2- to 3-kilometer route, which begins at a definite feature and traverses the terrain, passing over and along several distinct features. In the terrain, place streamers or markers en route, each with a letter or word that is part of a code. Do not mark the location of the streamers on the map.

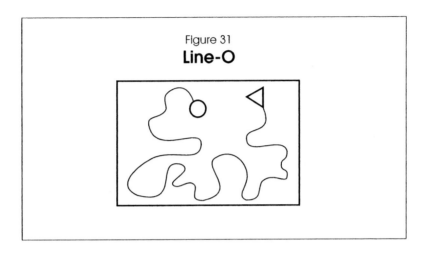

Figure 31
Line-O

Start: Orienteers, each armed with map and pencil, start at the triangle and try to follow the exact route indicated by the line on the map. If they stay on the line, they should find all the streamers in order. Write down each part of the code, put them together, and submit the word or phrase at the end.

Variations: (1) For extra map-reading practice, orienteers can mark the precise location of each streamer on their maps. (2) Use more conspicuous locations for novice orienteers.

12. Armchair-O (fig 32)

Goal: To learn to visualize terrain contours from the map

Means: Studying worksheets

Activity Level: Seated

Location: Indoor

Time Required: Ten to sixty minutes

Materials: Worksheets with contours and side-view illustrations, pencils

Preparation: Make up three to six worksheets that depict a simple contour drawing and one or more side-view drawings as possible matching choices, or draw the contour lines and leave room for the orienteer to draw the side view.

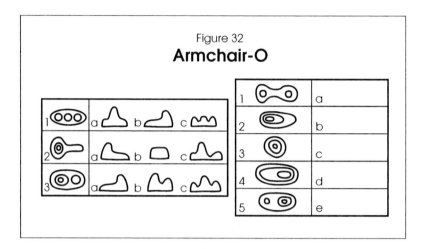

Figure 32
Armchair-O

Start: Pass out the worksheets to individuals or teams of orienteers. Explain how to do each sheet. Discuss choices and correct answers. See *Armchair Orienteering* by W. Stott for more exercises of this sort.

13. Map Walk: Contours and Water-Only Map

Goal: To isolate contours as map and terrain features in order to improve your ability to read and identify them

Means: Map walk and discussion

Activity Level: Walk

Location: Outdoor

Time Required: Thirty to sixty minutes

Materials: O-maps showing only contours and water—one map for each person

Preparation: Plan a map walk rich in contour features

Start: Walk as a group, maps in hand, reading as you go, stopping to discuss sizes, shapes, and distances of features in sight.

14. Map Walk: Estimating Size and Shape

Goal: To increase awareness of the relationship between the size and shape of a feature on a map and how it looks in the field

Means: Map walk and discussion

Activity Level: Walk

Location: Outdoor

Time Required: Thirty to sixty minutes

Materials: One map for each person

Preparation: Plan a map walk that will expose orienteers to features of different sizes, such as ponds, fields, hills, knolls, and boulders.

Start: Walk the terrain in a group, reading, pointing out, and discussing features as you go. Note height, area, shape, slope, and orientation of features. Encourage everyone to participate.

15. Landmark Hunt

Goal: To practice orienting a map and locating landmarks

Means: Identification of landmarks in terrain and on map

Activity Level: Walking/seated

Location: Outdoor

Materials: For each person: a topographic map, pencil, and list of ten landmarks to be located on the map

Preparation: Find a hill or some other high point of visibility and list the landmarks and their compass directions that the group will locate.

Start: On "Go," participants begin locating landmarks. The sequence might go like this:

1. Draw a circle on your map to indicate your present location.
2. Circle the mountain approximately southwest of here.
3. Circle the Y in the road north of here.
4. Circle the building approximately east-southeast of here.

16. Map Point Walk

Goal: To practice following a route and finding on a map the landmarks you see on the way

Activity Level: Walk

Location: Outdoor

Materials: Streamers, arrow markers, and a map and pencil for each person

Preparation: On a map, lay out an appropriate route of 3 kilometers, passing by several easily identifiable landmarks. Then go over the route in the field, marking it with colored streamers tied to trees, posts, or sticks, so that the next streamer can be seen from the preceding one. At some of the main landmarks, hang a much wider streamer (or a regular orienteering banner) and a north-pointing arrow marker to help the participants orient their maps.

Start: Participants, each with map and pencil, start every two minutes. The object is to follow the marked course and to put circles on the map to indicate the location of the streamers. Fastest time wins, if the landmark designations are correct. If some are incorrect, penalize by adding two to five minutes for each error.

17. Map Point Reporting

Goal: To practice map reading and improve powers of observation

Activity Level: Walk/run

Location: Outdoor

Preparation: Locate six to ten clearly identifiable landmarks over a 4- to 6-kilometer route, then hike to each one and make up a question, such as "What trees grow nearby?" or "What building can be seen?" The question can be correctly answered only by someone who visits the landmark.

Decide on a point value for each landmark.

Start: The participants leave two minutes apart, each with a map, a pencil, and a sheet that describes the location and point value of the landmarks and the questions to be answered. The object is to score the most points in a set amount of time, such as three hours. The best strategy might be to target the landmarks with the highest value first.

18. Fruit Relay

Goal: To enhance beginners' basic map-reading skills

Means: Fruit treasure hunt

Activity Level: Walk/run

Location: Outdoor

Time Required: Five to fifteen minutes

Materials: One orienteering or schoolyard map, one pencil for each person

Preparation: Ask each participant to bring a piece of fruit, which is uncut and large enough to fill the palm of your hand (not strawberries or grapes).

Start: On "Go," each person leaves the start area with map, pencil, and fruit, and places his or her piece of fruit somewhere that is distinct both on the map and in the terrain. The location is marked on the map with a circle. All participants return and exchange maps. On the second "Go," each person reads this new map to try to find the fruit in the circle. On returning, everyone eats the fruit.

Variations: (1) Use seasonal treats, such as valentines, Easter eggs, or Christmas candy. (2) If a large group is participating, each piece of fruit should have a code on it with a corresponding code placed on the map. This will verify that participants have found the correct fruit.

19. Flash Card Map Symbol Relay

Goal: To learn the international map symbols

Means: Relay race and flash card identification

Activity Level: Walk/run/seated

Location: Indoor/outdoor

Time Required: Ten to twenty minutes

Materials: Flash cards (5 x 7-inch index cards) with map symbol on one side and a written description of what the symbol stands for on the other side (see fig 33).

Preparation: For each group, make a set of ten to twenty flash cards. Divide participants into two or more groups and line them up. Stack the flash cards some distance away from the start, map symbol up.

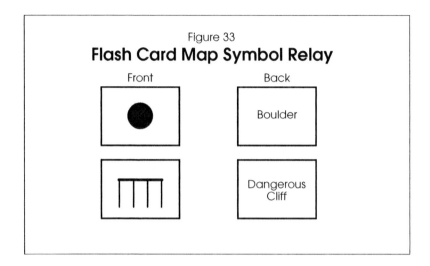

Figure 33
Flash Card Map Symbol Relay

Front   Back

Boulder

Dangerous Cliff

Start: On "Go," the lead on each team runs to the cards and quickly studies the first one. If he correctly identifies the map symbol, the card is placed in a separate pile; if he errs, the card is put at the bottom of the stack. Right or wrong, the runner races back and tags the next teammate. The winner is the first team to correctly identify all its cards.

Variation: This can also be played while seated, not unlike charades, with people shouting out the answers.

20. Thumbing

Goal: To learn to maintain awareness of one's position on the map

Means: Nature walk/run, moving thumb on map as location changes

Activity Level: Walk/run

Location: Outdoor

Time Required: Ten to twenty minutes

Materials: For each person, one map of a course of appropriate difficulty

Preparation: Decide on the course and provide each orienteer with a map.

Start: Do the course as a group, walking at first and then running if that's appropriate for the fitness level. Fold your map small enough (approximately 4 x 4 inches) so that your thumb can reach the center. Place your thumb at the start, and walk along noting distinct features that indicate current position. Move the thumb to each new identifiable position. Advanced orienteers should check beginners frequently for thumb position and map orientation.

21. Mapping a Room

Goal: To learn how maps present a two-dimensional top view of a space

Means: Mapping a room

Activity Level: Seated/walk

Location: Indoor

Time Required: Twenty to thirty minutes

Materials: One large sheet of paper or posterboard and one $8^1/_2$ x 11-inch sheet for each group

Preparation: Draw the perimeter of the room on the posterboard, indicating the locations of door and windows.

Start: Display the poster of the room perimeter. Identify the door and windows and generally orient yourselves. Each group takes a section of the room to map. Using paper and pencil, they should map their area in top view, as though there were no roof. Try drawing the objects to scale. When finished, each group should use a marker to transfer its section drawing to the posterboard. Use the finished map for further games and exercises.

22. Map Memory Under Stress

Goal: To exercise map memory under physical stress

Means: Drawing legs of a course from memory immediately after running that leg

Activity Level: Running

Location: Outdoor

Time Required: Ten to twenty minutes

Materials: Maps, paper, pencils, and a place to run a loop

Preparation: Draw several legs, not necessarily connected, on the map.

Start: Allow participants time (10, 20, 30 seconds) to study a leg, after which they run the leg. Upon returning, they immediately draw the leg from memory. Repeat, adjusting pace, and therefore fatigue level, to determine when proficiency falls.

23. Drawing Course in Review

Goal: To systematically evaluate your performance in order to determine which skills and techniques need improvement

Means: Drawing your actual route on your map after the race

Activity Level: Seated

Location: Indoor

Time Required: Ten to fifteen minutes

Materials: Course map, training diary, colored pen

Preparation: None

Start: Draw in the actual route you took as soon as it's convenient after you finish. Mark every stop. Make notes on the back of the map, leg by leg. Note whether attack points or catching features were used, whether the route choice was the best, and if not why not. Describe errors and how to avoid repeating them. Note in your training diary which patterns surface and which skills need improvement. File maps and notes, and refer to them before the next competition in the same area.

PACE AND DISTANCE ESTIMATION

24. Pacing 100 Meters

Goal: To determine one's pace while walking and running
Means: Walking/running 100 meters and counting steps
Activity Level: Walk/run
Location: Outdoor
Time Required: Five to seven minutes
Materials: Paper, pencils, and streamers or other means of marking 100 meters
Preparation: Measure 100 meters over flat, unobstructed terrain. Mark the start and finish with streamers or something else clearly visible.
Start: Participants line up on the starting line and walk to the finish, counting every double-step, beginning with zero. Record the walking result, and then try it again while jogging at a race pace.

25. Pacing Variations

Goals: To learn how slope and vegetation affect pacing
Means: Walking and running over various terrain
Activity Level: Walk/run
Location: Outdoor
Time Required: Fifteen to twenty minutes
Materials: Streamers, paper, pencils
Preparation: With streamers or controls, mark 100-meter courses in several areas—uphill and downhill, in the woods, through "slow-run" vegetation.
Start: Participants walk and run the various courses, counting their double-steps as paces. Record the results for the various conditions, add them to results from trail and road, and memorize them for estimating your distances in terrain.

26. Distance Estimation
Goal: To develop good distance judgment
Means: Estimating distances while running and walking
Activity Level: Walk/run
Location: Outdoor
Time Required: Any amount
Materials: None
Preparation: None
Start: When on the move, look ahead and estimate the distance between yourself and certain objects—tree, telephone pole, intersection. Then begin counting your double-steps to gauge the distance. Try again, adjusting your new estimation based on your old.

27. Map Walk: Estimating Size and Distance
Goal: To increase the ability to estimate the size of features or the distance between features
Means: Nature walk
Activity Level: Walk
Location: Outdoor
Time Required: Thirty to sixty minutes
Materials: One map for each person
Preparation: Select an area with just enough distinct features to allow identification of specific ones without confusion. Ideally, features should be within view and 50 to 300 meters apart or long.
Start: Walk with a group discussing the size of, or the distance between, distinct features. Stop frequently and estimate the height of a slope or the distance around the edge of a pond. Then pace to check your accuracy. Keep at it until you are fairly accurate.
Variation: Pick up the pace until you are accurate while running.

28. Feature Identification—Estimating Sizes and Distances

Goal: To improve the ability to estimate the size of, and the distance between, features

Means: Walk or run a course and choose the correct map at each control

Activity Level: Walk/run

Location: Outdoor

Time Required: Twenty to thirty minutes

Materials: Map, cardboard, streamer, knife, controls, paper, and pencils

Preparation: Select an area with six to ten features, each 50 to 300 meters long, such as fields, thickets, ponds, steep slopes, and cliffs. Cut out 1-inch-square pieces of map showing each feature, along with two other pieces of map showing a similar feature of different length or size. Mount all three on cards oriented to north. Then streamer a course from control feature to control feature. Hang the card with the three map squares at each control.

Start: Follow the streamers to each control. Observe the dimensions of each control feature, review the cards, and select the correct map. Record your answer and move on to the next control.

29. Compass and Pace Course

Goal: To increase proficiency with compass bearings and pace counting

Means: Course navigation with compass and bearing card

Activity Level: Walk

Location: Outdoor

Time Required: Twenty to thirty minutes

Materials: Streamers, marker, cards with bearings and distances, and one compass for each person

Preparation: Select an area of open woods. From a marked starting point, choose a bearing and pace off a distance of 30 to 50 meters. Mark this precise location with a streamer, give it a code, and write its bearing and distance on a card. Then hang additional streamers in the area, all with codes and far enough away to avoid confusion with the proper control. Select four to six additional target points to complete the course, repeating the streamering process at each. Make up one card for each participant with bearings and distances to each point.

Start: Each person should have a compass and a card with bearings and distances. Use compass and pacing to navigate to the first streamered area, record the code of what you believe is the correct streamer, calculate the next bearing, and move on to the second control.

COMPASS USE

30. Using a Compass as a Protractor
Goal: To increase one's understanding of the use of the compass as protractor

Means: Measuring and drawing an angle on paper

Activity Level: Seated

Location: Indoor/outdoor

Time Required: Fifteen minutes

Materials: One compass per one or two people

Preparation: Know that a protractor-style compass can be used to measure an angle—that is, the location of a feature with respect to due north.

Start: Draw a 120-degree angle on a piece of posterboard. Hold it level, and note how the angle can be rotated to face any direction (although it was drawn oriented to north). Use your compass to find north, and then turn your whole body (and the poster) until the north end of the needle is in the gate and the north end of the poster points north. Now point to the feature that is at 120 degrees.

31. Running on Rough Compass
Goal: To learn to run quickly in a given direction without taking an exact bearing

Means: Finding a target in the terrain with only a rough bearing

Activity Level: Running
Location: Outdoor
Time Required: Twenty to thirty minutes
Materials: One compass for each person, cards, streamers
Preparation: Select an area with good runnability and distinct features. Set a course with six to ten legs, using a map to verify compass bearings and distances to features. Each leg should be 50 to 200 meters long and end at a distinct feature, from which a streamer is hung. For each leg, record the rough bearing, the distance to the feature, and the type of feature. For example, the first line might read "NE 75m boulder," indicating that the first leg goes northeast for 75 meters to a boulder.

Start: Each participant has one card and one compass. The object is to run as fast as possible on a rough compass bearing for the distance given. Stagger the start. Runners should look at the compass often. A streamer will identify the target feature. You must find the streamer before moving on to the next leg.

Variation: Compete as teams.

ORIENTEERING TECHNIQUE
Rough Orienteering

32. Handrail and Large Feature Course

Goal: To learn to move quickly through the terrain by using handrails and large features

Means: Map reading and terrain interpretation

Activity Level: Running

Location: Outdoor

Time Required: Thirty to sixty minutes

Materials: One map for each person, control descriptions, control cards, control markers

Preparation: Select an area with large features and both subtle and obvious handrails. Design a course that allows participants to follow handrails of appropriate difficulty, and use large features for the greater part of each leg. Set markers for the controls, which should be easy to find. Mark maps and control descriptions. Review definition of handrail and discuss various types, such as waterways, contour differences, changes in vegetation.

Start: Distribute maps and stagger the start. Emphasize the use of handrails to move quickly and get close to the controls.

Variation: Have assistant coaches or veteran orienteers position themselves along the course to evaluate the participants' use of handrails.

33. Map Simplification—Drawing a Course

Goal: To learn to view the map's larger features and commit them to memory in order to move quickly through the terrain

Means: Map reading, map memory, and map simplification

Activity Level: Walk/run

Location: Outdoor

Time Required: Sixty to ninety minutes

Materials: Paper, colored pencils, and one map for each person; control markers

Preparation: Design a short (3-kilometer) course with four or five legs with both large features (hills, streams, clearings) and fine details (boulders, thickets, small marshes). Legs should permit participants to navigate by large features. Draw the course on the maps.

Start: Participants copy down a simplified version of the course. Then they head out to find controls, aided only by their simplified maps. They may take the real maps as backups in case they get lost.

Fine Orienteering

34. Control Picking Course

Goal: To learn fine map reading and use of attack points when approaching a control

Means: Precision map reading

Activity Level: Walk/run

Location: Outside

Time Required: Twenty to thirty minutes

Materials: One map for each person, control descriptions, control markers

Preparation: Select an area with a lot of detail. Design a short course (2 kilometers) with six to ten controls placed 200 to 300 meters apart. Hang controls, mark maps.

Start: Participants use each control as an attack point for finding the next control. Stagger the start. Go as fast as possible while reading the map. Review when finished.

Mastering Control Descriptions

35. Connect the Dots

Goal: To learn to quickly identify and interpret control symbols on clue sheets and control appearance on maps

Means: Identifying controls from descriptions on clue sheets

Activity Level: Seated

Location: Indoor

Time Required: Ten to fifteen minutes

Materials: Pens and one map for each person, with a course of appropriate difficulty drawn on it. Show only the start triangle and the control circles—no lines or control numbers.

Preparation: Design courses of appropriate difficulty, making sure that each control location lends itself to a unique description. Mark the maps with the circles and start triangle only. Devise an IOF control description sheet for each map.

Start: Each player has a pen, map, and clue sheet. On "Go," players use their clue sheets to figure out which control is first, which is second, and so on. They should draw a line from the start triangle to the first control, from the first control to the second, and so on until all controls have been identified and numbered. First correct finisher wins.

36. Control Description Identification

Goal: To increase ability to recognize IOF control description symbols

Means: Flash card exercises

Activity Level: Seated

Location: Indoor

Time Required: Ten to twenty minutes

Materials: Paper, pencils, and flash cards (5 x 7-inch index cards) with control descriptions displayed in eight-column IOF format (fig 34).

Preparation: On one side of ten to fifteen index cards, draw control descriptions, using IOF symbols large enough to be seen at 10 meters. On the other side, write an interpretation of that description, such as "Between two boulders, one of which is 2 meters high, the other 3 meters high."

Start: Participants number their papers 1 through 10 or 15. As the symbol sides of the flash cards are shown one at a time, participants write a description for each card. When finished, review the cards and discuss.

Figure 34
IOF Symbols for Control Descriptions

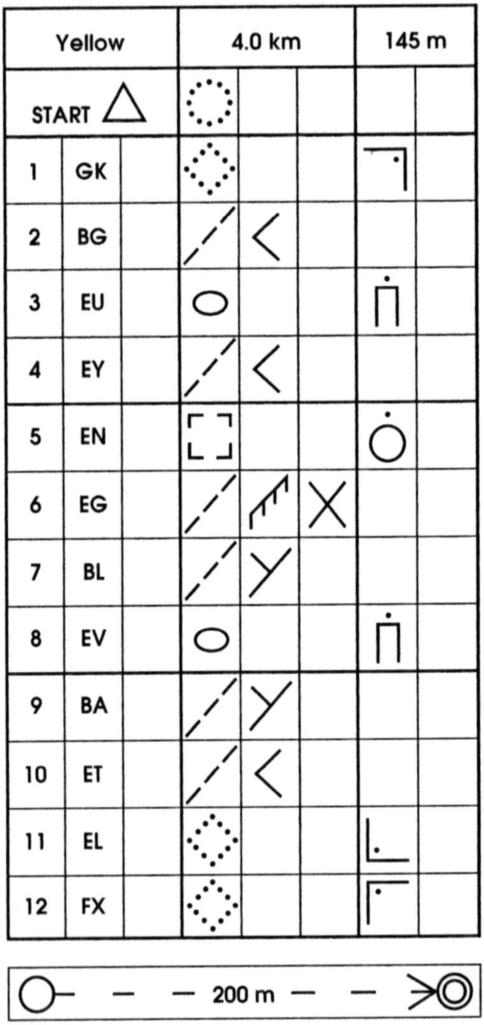

Yellow		4.0 km			145 m
START △	◌				
1	GK	◌			⌐•
2	BG	╱	‹		
3	EU	○			∏̇
4	EY	╱	‹		
5	EN	⌐⌐			Ȯ
6	EG	╱	⌓	✕	
7	BL	╱	⅄		
8	EV	○			∏̇
9	BA	╱	⅄		
10	ET	╱	‹		
11	EL	◇			⌐•
12	FX	◇			⌐

○— — — 200 m — — ⟩◎

Safety bearing: 180° north

Route Planning

37. Leap Frog

Goal: To improve the ability to plan a route while on the run

Means: Running in the lead, then following another leader

Activity Level: Run

Location: Outside

Time Required: Twenty to thirty minutes

Materials: Controls, one map for each person

Preparation: Come up with a short course (2 to 3 kilometers) with eight to ten legs featuring route choices.

Start: Divide the group into pairs of like ability. Stagger the start. At "Go," the two teammates go off toward control No. 1, one of them leading, running continuously and map reading on the run; the second follows, planning the second leg on the run. At control No. 1, the teammates switch positions, with the new follower now planning the third leg on the run. Alternate in this way for the entire course.

This tends to be a fast drill, as each new leader already has a route planned and simply needs to execute it. When finished, discuss route choices.

38. Comparing Route Choices

Goal: To determine when to use trails and when to go cross-country

Means: Running both the trail and the cross-country route of legs

Activity Level: Run

Location: Outside

Time Required: Sixty to seventy-five minutes

Materials: One map for each person, control markers, pens, stopwatches, index cards

Preparation: Select an area with a simple trail network. Pick out legs that offer a choice between running cross-country and running a trail. Both routes should share the same start and the same finish. Set the controls, put index cards at each control, and mark the maps.

Start: Make sure everyone understands that the course is to be run twice. Stagger starts. At "Go," participants receive a map and an index card and head cross-country toward the first control. At each control, record the time of arrival on the card. At the finish, record the time and initials.

After a rest, get a new card and do the course again, this time choosing the trail option on each leg. When finished, compare the times on each leg. Look at the map to determine what variables dictate choosing one option over the other.

Attack Points

39. Finding Attack Points

Goal: To learn to recognize attack points
Means: Map reading, drawing
Activity Level: Seated
Location: Inside
Time Required: Fifteen minutes
Materials: One pencil, one map for each person
Preparation: Select a course on a map with many attack point possibilities. The course should have about a dozen legs, with distances of 150 meters to 700 meters each. Select control locations that have one or more attack points and a route choice. Attack points should be within 150 meters of the control.

Start: Participants plan each leg, beginning by selecting an attack point and circling it in pencil. Then select a route to reach the attack point and draw that in. When all legs are completed, discuss.

Variation: Do the activity in pairs or groups.

Collecting Features

40. Finding Collecting/Catching Features

Goal: To improve the ability to recognize collecting and catching features

Means: Highlighting such features on a map

Activity Level: Seated

Location: Inside

Time Required: Ten to fifteen minutes

Materials: One map and one highlighting pen for each person

Preparation: Select a map rich in linear features that has beginner courses on it. Most legs should have at least one collecting feature (before control) and catching feature (after control).

Start: Each player highlights collecting and catching features on each leg. Discuss leg by leg or when the entire course is completed.

Variation: Do the exercise in pairs.

QUIZZES

Answers to quizzes can be found on page 177

41. Direction Quiz

Goal: To practice calculating degree directions on a map using an orienteering compass

Activity Level: Seated

Location: Indoor

Time Required: Ten minutes

Materials: Orienteering compass, map, paper, and pencil for each person

Start: Referring to the map in figure 35, use your orienteering compass to calculate the directions in degrees between the following points:

1. From intersection of Jansen Trail and Elizabeth Road to Hillamanjaro _____ degrees.
2. From intersection of Jansen Trail and Elizabeth Road to The Old Hollister Place _____ degrees.
3. From Ye Old Bone Yard to St. Barbara and Bill's Church _____ degrees.

Figure 35

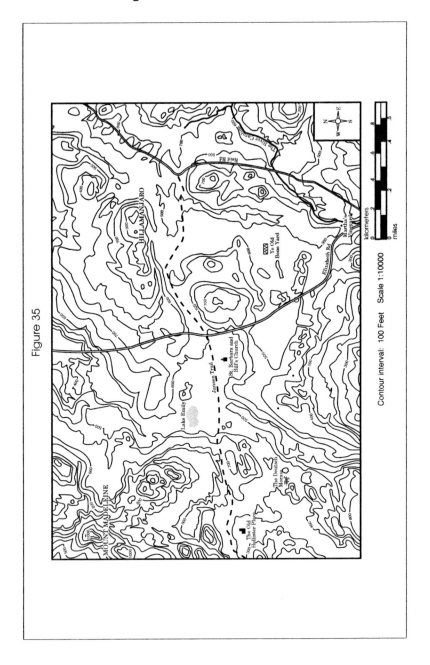

Contour interval: 100 Feet   Scale 1:10000

4. From Hillamanjaro to the intersection of Reid Road and Jansen Trail _____ degrees.

5. From Martha's Vineyard to Ye Old Bone Yard _____ degrees.

Variation: Play it as a game. Orally give the directions to the group: "What is the direction in degrees from . . . to . . .?" As soon as a player has the answer, she holds up her hand. If correct within five degrees, she scores twenty points; if wrong, the question is still up for grabs.

42. Distance Quiz

Goal: To practice measuring distances on a map

Activity Level: Seated

Location: Indoor

Materials: Copies of a map

Preparation: Cut out the scale rule on the map and transfer it to the edge of a piece of paper or cardboard strip, or use a ruler or the straight edge of your orienteering compass.

Start: Using your compass or the cardboard strip, determine the crow-flight distance, expressed in kilometers, between the following points on the map in figure 35.

1. From The Old Hollister Place to Hillamanjaro _____

2. From Jansen Trail and Elizabeth Road to St. Barbara and Bill's Church _____

3. From Lake Emily to The Old Hollister Place _____

4. From St. Barbara and Bill's Church to Ye Old Bone Yard

   _____

5. From Lake Emily to Mount Madeleine _____

Variation: To play this as a game, each player should have an orienteering compass or the cardboard strip with the scale on it. The leader asks for a distance, and the first player with the correct answer within 50 meters scores twenty points.

43. Compass Setting Quiz

Goal: To become familiar with setting the orienteering compass for different directions on the map

Activity Level: Seated

Location: Indoor

Materials: Map, compass, pencil, and list of bearings to find

Start: Break out the compass, open up the map (fig 35), and take an imaginary walk. Start at The Old Hollister Place and determine the bearing to each new location:

1. From The Old Hollister Place to the southwestern shore of Lake Emily _____
2. From the southwestern shore of Lake Emily to Mount Madeleine _____
3. From Mount Madeleine to The Deutsch Morass _____
4. From The Deutsch Morass to St. Barbara and Bill's Church _____
5. From St. Barbara and Bill's Church to Martha's Vineyard _____
6. From Martha's Vineyard back to The Old Hollister Place _____

Variation: Make a game out of this exercise.

44. What Do You Find?

Goal: To practice making correct bearing measurements and translating them into compass directions

Activity Level: Seated

Location: Indoor

Start: Using your compass and the map in figure 35, determine the bearing and compass direction of the following features relative to St. Barbara and Bill's Church.

1. To Ye Old Bone Yard _____
2. To the intersection of Jansen Trail and Elizabeth Road _____

3. To Martha's Vineyard _____
4. To The Old Hollister Place _____
5. To the northern map end of Elizabeth Road _____

Variation: Make it a game. Each player has a map, compass, pencil, and list of the above. Players have ten minutes to finish the task. Score ten points for each correct bearing and ten points for each correct compass direction.

(Answers to Direction Quiz: 1. 46, 2. 254, 3. 280, 4. 135, 5. 335)

(Answers to Distance Quiz: 1. 1.7 km, 2. .15 km, 3. .6 km, 4. .6 km, 5. .8 km)

(Answers to Compass Setting Quiz: 1. 70 degrees, 2. 310, 3. 165, 4. 60, 5. 135, 6. 286)

(Answers to What Do You Find?: 1. 112 degrees ESE, 2. 52 degrees NE, 3. 138 degrees SE, 4. 262 degrees W, 5. 6 degrees N)

GLOSSARY

aerobic exercise: a continuous, rhythmic exercise during which the body's oxygen needs are still being met. Aerobic activities include brisk walking, running, swimming, cycling, and cross-country skiing. A conditioned athlete can carry on aerobic exercise for a long time (in contrast to *anaerobic exercise).*

age-group: competition separated by age. Orienteering offers many age groups, including 12–13, 14–15, 16–17, 18–19, and senior classifications in five-year increments over 35.

agonic line: a line of zero declination that runs east of Florida and through Lake Michigan.

aiming off: a navigational technique whereby one intentionally aims right or left of a target. If, for example, you are returning to your car parked on a road, you might aim 10 degrees to the right of your calculated bearing, so that when you reach the road, you know that your car lies to the left.

anaerobic exercise: exercise at an intensity level that exceeds the ability of the body to dispose of the lactic acid produced by the muscles. As a result, this exercise can be sustained for only a short time before exhaustion sets in. Examples of anaerobic exercise include weight lifting, sprinting, and calisthenics.

anaerobic threshold: the point in an exercise at which further increase in effort will cause more lactic acid to accumulate than can be readily eliminated. Past this point, the body is working so hard that it is unable to supply enough oxygen for the muscle cells to work efficiently. Competitive orienteers can operate near their anaerobic threshold.

attack point: a feature on the map that is within about 100 meters of the control and easy to locate. The idea is for the orienteer to use rough orienteering to find the attack point quickly, then use fine orienteering over a small area to find the control.

back bearing: the direction, or bearing, of a visible landmark behind your direction of travel.

ballistic stretching: quick, bouncing stretches that force muscles to lengthen. The muscles react by reflexively contracting or shortening, increasing the likelihood of muscle tears and soreness.

base: one's endurance level, which is raised by running many miles at an aerobic level.

baseplate: the rectangular, transparent plate on which the orienteering compass housing is mounted. A direction-of-travel arrow and ruled edges are engraved on the baseplate.

bearing: in orienteering, the direction relative to magnetic north.

belly breathing: the proper abdominal breathing technique in which the belly expands as you breathe in and flattens as you breathe out.

blow up: to overexert and sap oneself of energy and concentration.

cardinal points: the four principal points of the compass: north, south, east, and west.

cartography: map making.

catching feature: a feature, such as a road, fence, or hillside, that is usually beyond the control and perpendicular to your route. It catches the attention of the orienteer who has traveled beyond the control and tells her that she has gone too far. It is sometimes useful to overshoot the control deliberately, hit the catching feature, and approach the control from behind.

clearing: a small treeless area found in forests.

collapse point: the point in a race where you can go no farther. In distance, it is usually reached at about three times your daily average.

collecting feature: a feature, such as a reentrant or pond, that crosses your path between you and the control and is used to funnel you or direct you along the way.

compass: a handheld tool for determining direction, featuring a magnetized needle suspended on a point in a compass housing marked in 360 degrees.

contact: relating the ground to the map and vice versa. Being "in contact" means being accurately located.

contouring: running or walking along a slope while remaining at the same elevation, that is, on the same contour. Line-O is a good technique for developing this skill.

contour interval: the difference in elevation between one contour line and the one next to it, usually 5 meters. On a map of a rather level area, however, the contour interval may be as little as 2.5 meters.

contour line: a line on a topographic map, any point of which is the same elevation above sea level. The line indicating the boundary of a lake could be on a contour line.

control card: a card carried by the orienteer and punched at each control to verify her visit.

control circle: a circle 6 millimeters in diameter centered on each feature on an orienteering course that is the location of a control.

control code: a two- or three-digit or two-letter symbol on the control marker that identifies the control.

control description: a short explanation, following a specific format, of what the feature looks like where you can expect to find the control marker. In English, it might read, "Boulder, south side." International control descriptions are symbolic to transcend language barriers.

control extension: a map-reading technique that "enlarges" the control feature to include other features in the area, thereby creating a larger target for the orienteer to hit. For example, a boulder, which is the control feature, sits on a spur, and the spur becomes the larger target.

control flow: the fluency of arriving at, punching, and moving away from a control marker. Top orienteers typically take only three to four seconds at the control.

control marker: the three-dimensional orange-and-white nylon flag used to mark the control feature.

control number: the number beside each control circle on the map that indicates the order in which the controls are supposed to be visited. It is also listed on the description sheet and corresponds to the number on the control card.

cool-down: an important final phase of exercise during which the rate of physical exertion, and hence the heart, is gradually decreased.

course: the start, controls, and finish visited by each orienteering competitor. Several different courses are set out at each event.

cramping: painful contraction of muscles caused by the loss of potassium and other minerals during the excessive sweating of exercise.

cross-bearings: two or more bearings that, when plotted on a map, indicate your position where they cross (see *triangulation*).

cross-country: running or walking that is both off-road and off-trail.

cross-training: regularly performing more than one aerobic activity, thus exercising different muscle groups and providing variety. Interspersing running with biking and swimming—as triathletes do—is an example of cross-training.

cultural features: man-made landscape features, such as roads, buildings, and walls.

dampen: to slow down or deaden the oscillation of a compass needle. In liquid damping, the most common method, this is achieved by filling the compass housing with oil.

daypack: a medium-sized soft pack, favored by day hikers, for carrying food, water, and other supplies; bigger than a fanny pack, smaller than a backpack.

declination (variation): the difference in degrees between magnetic north, where the compass needle points, and true north, which is the top of most maps. Orienteers don't have to worry about declination, as their maps are drawn to magnetic north.

dehydration: a depletion of body fluids that can hinder the body's ability to regulate its temperature. One can become dehydrated during exercise if the fluids lost through perspiration are not replaced by drinking water. Chronic dehydration lowers an athlete's tolerance to fatigue, reduces her ability to sweat, elevates rectal temperature, and increases stress on the circulatory system. In general, a loss of 2 percent or more of one's body weight by sweating affects performance; a loss of 5 percent to 6 percent affects health.

detraining: the reduction of fitness level because of inactivity. Studies have found that physical fitness (as measured by endurance, changes in maximum heart rate, and other criteria) declines rapidly in the first twelve days of inactivity and then continues to decline, though not as rapidly. However, even after three months of not exercising, these erstwhile athletes were still fitter than people who had never exercised.

direction: the line a moving person takes, usually expressed in terms of left, right, or straight, relative to the control or a prominent feature.

direction-of-travel arrow: the arrow etched onto the baseplate that indicates which way you should go.

DNF: racer's shorthand for "did not finish."

DQ: disqualified.

electrolytes: minerals in food and drink; potassium, magnesium, and sodium are the most important for endurance athletes because they are sweated away quickly.

endorphins: opiate-like substances produced by the central nervous system that suppress pain. These natural pain relievers seem to be released during vigorous exercise.

endurance: the ability to withstand pain, stress, or fatigue and keep going.

ergogenic aid: any stimulant or artificial aid used to improve athletic performance. Just about all are illegal for competition, except the caffeine in coffee.

exercise physiology: the study of the workings of the body during activity.

exercise stress test: an electrocardiogram taken while you are exercising.

fanny pack: a small, soft pack worn around the waist, to hold a few emergency supplies.

fartlek: a Swedish term meaning "speed play," it is a type of interval training in which the runner alternates sprinting with relaxed running. A clock is not used; instead, the runner sprints for a certain distance or toward a chosen object, such as a telephone pole. The technique lacks structure in pace and intensity but can be a useful training aid for the disciplined runner.

fell: a hill or mountain. This term is obscure except in the proper names of hills in northern England, where fell running is popular.

field: on an orienteering map, an area enclosed by a boundary in which crops or grass is growing.

fight: impenetrable or extremely difficult forest or brush, indicated by dark green on orienteering maps. Generally to be avoided.

fine orienteering: moving slowly and keeping in touch with where you are on the map at all times. Small terrain features are used along the way to check your position on the map. Slow and inefficient for an entire leg, it is ideal when nearing a control.

finish symbol: a double circle that marks the location of a finish area on a map.

fitness: ability to put one's health to work in a dynamic way. One can be healthy without being fit, but not the reverse.

flexibility: the ability of the joints to move through their full range of motion. Good flexibility protects muscles and ligaments from pulls and tears.

glucose: the sugar that results when carbohydrates are converted to glycogen for storage. Because drinks made of glucose solutions require relatively little work to digest, they are commonly used by serious endurance athletes.

gorp: a high-carbohydrate snack food made primarily from nuts and dried fruit; an acronym for "good ol' raisins and peanuts."

handrail: linear feature used to guide an orienteer along a route. Beginner's courses are designed to use handrails, such as trails, streams, fences, and power lines. For intermediate and advanced courses, the handrails are usually more subtle, such as ridges or distinct changes in contour spacing.

heat cramps: a knotting of muscles—typically calf, arms, and abdomen—usually caused by prolonged exercise in hot weather.

heat exhaustion: a debilitating ailment, the symptoms of which may include headache, dizziness, nausea, gooseflesh, rubbery legs, fainting, a weak but rapid pulse, muscle cramps, and a hot, flushed feeling around the head and shoulders. Though rarely fatal, it can precede potentially fatal heatstroke.

heatstroke: the most severe of the three heat ailments. It causes con-

fusion, loss of neuromuscular control, unconsciousness, and per-
ilously high body temperatures—more than 104 degrees.

housing: the rotatable portion of an orienteering compass that contains the needle.

hydrographic features: water features, such as lakes, rivers, and
marshes, that are printed in blue on topographic maps.

hypsographic features: elevation features—mountains, hills, valleys, and plains—that are printed in brown on topographic
maps.

index pointer: the line on the baseplate of the orienteering compass
against which the degree number on the dial of the compass
housing is read.

interval training: a way of exercising that alternates spurts of
intense exertion with lower-intensity periods in one exercise session.

in the gate: phrase for when the compass needle is directly over the
orienting arrow in the housing, pointing toward *N*.

jogging: movement that is in between walking and running. It's
debatable exactly where jogging ends and running begins, but
Dr. Kenneth Cooper defines jogging as movement that is slower
than nine minutes per mile.

junior: an age-group category that in orienteering includes participants younger than twenty-one.

K: abbreviation for kilometer, as in 7-K orienteering course.

kick: the acceleration at the end of a run or race.

kilometer: one thousand meters ($5/8$ of a mile).

knoll: small hill or mound, usually indicated on a topo map by a
brown dot or small, single-ring contour.

lactic acid: a by-product of anaerobic exercise that accumulates in
the muscles, causing pain and fatigue.

landmark: a geographical (natural or man-made) feature that can
help an orienteer relocate himself.

latitude: imaginary lines that run parallel to the equator and measure, in degrees, the distance north and south from the equator.

leg: the section of the course between controls. The start to the first
control is the first leg, and so on.

legend: a map's dictionary that explains the meaning of the symbols and colors used on the map. There is a standard legend that applies to all orienteering maps.

ligaments: tough bands of elastic tissue that join bones together to prevent excessive movement; source of many running injuries.

linear feature: a narrow natural or man-made feature, such as a fence, stream, or path, that extends for some distance.

longitude: imaginary lines that run from pole to pole and measure, in degrees, the distance east and west from Greenwich, England.

magnetic north: the direction a compass needle always points.

magnetic north lines: parallel north-south lines shown on all orienteering maps.

map: a reduced representation of a portion of the surface of the earth. The modern orienteering map maker uses aerial photography, which is checked by surveys in the field. Most maps are now drawn and printed with the aid of a computer.

map memory: systematically committing to memory map information to minimize the number of times the orienteer has to look at the map.

map symbols: printed marks or pictures that represent real terrain features.

master maps: maps displayed near the start showing the course, which competitors copy onto their own maps. This often occurs after the start and is therefore included in the total running time.

maximum heart rate (MHR): the highest heart rate you can achieve during your greatest exercise effort. MHR, computed by subtracting your age from 220, is used to calculate your training heart rate (THR).

meridian (longitude) lines: lines on a map that run true north to true south, lines that, extended far enough, would hit the North Pole in one direction and the South Pole in the other. The numbers attached to these lines are degrees of longitude, measured westward from the zero-degree line that runs through Greenwich, England.

muscular endurance: the ability to perform repeated muscular contractions in rapid succession, as in weight-lifting repetitions.

muscular strength: the force a muscle produces in one exertion, such as a jump.

niche: a hollow in a hillside slope, indicated by an indent in a single contour.

orient: to set the map in agreement with the points of the compass.

orienteering: a cross-country sport in forested and unknown terrain in which competitors, using only a compass and a detailed map, attempt to find the fastest route between a series of flagged checkpoints called controls.

orienteering compass: a compass especially designed to simplify the act of finding your way with map and compass. Its compass housing is mounted on a transparent baseplate in such a way that it can be turned easily.

orienting arrow: an arrow engraved on the bottom of the compass housing; used for setting the compass.

orienting the map: lining up the directions of the map with the same directions in the field. This can be done by inspection of features or by using a compass.

orthotic: a custom-made support worn inside shoes to compensate for arch defects and other biomechanical imbalances in the feet and legs.

overcompensation injury: pain caused by the tendency to favor one part of the body to protect another part of the body.

overtraining: any intense training to which the body cannot adapt and that results in physical and mental fatigue not easily overcome.

overuse: doing too much too fast; the cause of most running injuries.

oxygen debt: the condition that occurs when the oxygen needs of working muscles exceed the available supply, causing feelings of breathlessness and muscular fatigue. Exercise that results in oxygen debt is called "anaerobic."

oxygen uptake: a measurement of the amount of oxygen the body processes during exercise; a good measurement of endurance fitness.

pace: rate of running speed. Distance runners measure it in minutes per mile, as in "five-minute miles," while sprinters are more likely to speak in terms of, say, "sixty-second quarters," and orienteers in terms of, say, "sixty double-strides per hundred meters."

pace-work: practice-running at a pace one wishes to maintain in a race. If your goal is to run at an eight-minute-per-mile pace, doing quarters in two minutes each would be pace-work, while 100-second quarters would be speed work.

pacing: in orienteering, the measurement of distance while navigating. It is done by counting steps, usually two at a time.

peak: a period of time when the mind and body are operating at a maximum performance level. Some athletes have peak seasons, others peak moments.

peaking: simultaneously reaching a physical and emotional high point.

pedometer: a small instrument for measuring the distance walked or run. Pedometers and similar instruments are not allowed in orienteering (see *pacing*).

photogrammetry: use of air photography for surveying.

pickups: increases in pace—sprints—within longer runs; used for training purposes.

planimetric map: map that does not indicate contour, in contrast to *topographic map.*

plantar fascia: a thick, padlike band of tissue along the bottom of the foot. Stress to this area from excessive running or jumping can cause plantar fasciitis.

plantar fasciitis: an inflammation of the connective tissue that runs from the base of the toes to the heel bone; an overuse injury.

power-walking: walking at a pace that rivals slow running, usually between four and five miles per hour. The physical-psychological benefits of this activity are much the same as for running.

PR: personal record, or the best time for an individual over a particular course. It is the most significant record for most of us, as it allows us to compete against our former selves.

predicted maximum heart rate: the maximum number of times a person's heart should beat per minute when running full out, factoring in age and state of fitness. Used in calculating *target heart rate.*

prestart: call-up time, usually one to three minutes before your start time.

protractor: a device for reading angles. You can use the modern orienteering compass as a protractor.

pulled muscle: a tear in the muscle fiber. Proper warm-up is a good defense, as flexible muscles are less likely to tear.

punch: a small clipper with a distinctive arrangement of pins located at each control and used by orienteers to mark their control cards. The pattern of needles is different at each control. Electronic punches are replacing the needle punch at elite events in Europe.

quadrangle: a USGS map.

recovery heart rate: the goal of the post-exercise cool-down. A leisurely five-minute walk after a run should bring your pulse down below 120 beats per minute, below 110 if you are more than fifty years old. After an additional five minutes of stretching and relaxing exercises, your pulse should be within twenty beats of your pre-exercise resting heart rate.

reentrant: a small concave area, usually without a stream. In hilly terrain, this is a minor side valley, usually off a main valley.

relocation: finding your position after losing it by such techniques as determining the last accurate location, thinking about what you've seen, what direction you've traveled, and how far you've run.

repetition: each hard workout in an interval workout.

resection: determining a location by cross-bearings (see *triangulation*).

resistance work: training with extra "drag," such as in sand or up hills or with extra weight.

resting heart rate (RHR): the number of heartbeats per minute while the body is at rest; most accurately measured by taking your pulse before rising in the morning.

rough compass: running on a compass bearing or on the needle with little precision in keeping to the line of travel. It is usually combined with rough orienteering.

rough orienteering: the technique whereby the orienteer peruses the map for a general idea where and how far to go—for example, west-northwest, 400 meters—then runs to a collecting feature. Orienteers use this technique during the first part of the leg to move quickly to an area at which they can pinpoint their location. It relies on large terrain features such as swamps, fields, and hillsides (contrast with *fine orienteering*).

route choice: a basic element of orienteering strategy in which the competitor selects the optimum route between controls.

runnability: a description of the terrain in terms of how easy it is to run through. It is classified on orienteering maps by color or other symbols.

saddle: a narrow area between a knoll and a hill or another knoll.

safety direction: a compass bearing to guide lost orienteers to a road or major trail.

scale: the proportion between map distance and real distance. On a 1:10,000-scale map, for example, one unit on the map equals 10,000 of those same units on the ground.

set: in interval training, a specific number of repetitions of an exercise.

Silva: trademark of Silva Industries, used to identify orienteering and other high-grade compasses, as well as other orienteering equipment.

slope: the gradient of a rise or fall, or how much it deviates from the horizontal.

specificity: a theory in athletic training that says athletes become proficient at the specific tasks they practice.

speed work: training at a pace faster than you intend to race. Intervals and fartleks are two common types of speed work. Even ultramarathoners, who run 50- and 100-mile races, do weekly speed work.

sports medicine: a burgeoning branch of medicine dealing with the strains, sprains, and sicknesses incurred by people who recreate vigorously.

sprain: an injury that damages a ligament or ligaments, as well as joint capsules. Sprains can be mild, moderate, or severe, the latter meaning that one or more ligaments is completely torn.

sprint: a short burst of speed by a runner vying for the finish line or by an orienteer in between controls.

sprinter's hill: a steep hill that is short enough to be climbed quickly, without hindrance from muscular bulk.

spur: a small but distinct convex form on a slope, often used as a control. In hilly country, a minor ridge that erupts from a main ridge. It is often flanked by reentrants.

stamina: resistance to fatigue, illness, and hardship; staying power.

steady state: the dividing line between aerobic (normal breathing) and anaerobic (out-of-breath) running; as fitness improves, the pace at which one can run in a "steady state" increases.

stitch: a sharp pain in the side, believed to be a spasm of the diaphragm muscle that separates the lungs from the abdomen. Causes include breathing from the chest instead of the belly, and eating just before exercising.

straight-line route: the shortest route between control points.

strain: a stretched or partially torn muscle. Strains often occur when muscles suddenly and powerfully contract. Factors contributing to strains include poor conditioning, fatigue, weakness, and inadequate or improper warm-up. The leg, groin, and shoulder are the most common sites for strains.

strength: the capacity for resisting stress and strain.

stress: what you put your body through when you exercise; the right amount of stress is necessary for improvement, but too much causes the body to break down.

stress injury: an exercise-related injury, usually caused by the wear and tear of performing a repetitive activity.

stretching: slow, steady exercises that improve the flexibility of tendons, ligaments, and muscles (see *yoga*).

String course: short course for kids under ten that is marked in the terrain by continuous string or tape or by a series of streamers.

stub: the part of the control card that at some events is handed in at the prestart. It is used to record who is out on the course and for displaying the results at the end.

tactics: strategy used in racing to gain steps on opponents.

tapering: cutting back on mileage before an event; racers taper from a day to a week before a big race.

target heart rate: the heart rate during exercise in which the greatest training benefit occurs; usually 65 percent to 85 percent of the predicted maximum heart rate.

tendinitis: an inflammation of a tendon, causing pain and swelling. Most common site in runners and orienteers is the Achilles tendon above the heel.

tendons: the cords of connective tissue that anchor muscles to bones.

thumbing: a map-reading technique in which the map is folded into an approximate 4- by 4-inch square or small enough so that the participant's thumb can reach the center of the folded map to mark her present location. The thumb moves along the map to reflect the changing position of the orienteer.

topographic (topo) map: a map that uses contour lines, which connect points of equal elevation, to show the shape of the land, or topography.

training: working out now for some future reward, such as fitness or personal records; the process of applying the proper quantity and quality of stress.

training effect: the positive physiological changes that can be brought on by intense, continuous exercise. These include increased number and size of blood vessels, increased lung capacity, reduction of body fat, improved muscle tone, and lowered resting pulse.

training heart rate (THR): the aerobic heart rate; the rate that provides sufficient training effect for your cardiovascular system. This target zone of safe, beneficial training falls between two numbers, the target rate of 65 percent or 70 percent of your maximum heart rate and the cut-off figure of 85 percent of maximum heart rate.

treadmill stress test (TMST): a procedure to determine a person's degree of fitness and cardiovascular health. In a properly conducted stress test, the subject walks to exhaustion on a treadmill with a moving, motorized belt.

triangulation: a method of determining your position whereby bearings are taken to two visible landmarks. You are located where the two lines cross.

variation: another term for declination.

vegetation: features of the flora relevant to navigation or runnability. It is shown on orienteering maps by color and shade. For example, white is runnable trees, green is less runnable, and yellow is open ground and fields with no trees. The boundary between two distinct types of vegetation is shown by a black dotted line.

warm-up: pre-workout activities, such as walking, jogging, and stretching, designed to get the body heated up and ready to go.

weight-bearing exercise: exercise in which the legs support the body, such as walking, running, and jumping rope.

weight training: lifting barbells and dumbbells to increase strength and correct muscular imbalances.

wind chill: the cooling of the body that results from wind passing over its surface—especially dramatic if the surface is wet. It is a more useful measurement of meteorological discomfort than is temperature alone.

yoga: gentle, slow-moving stretching exercises; ideal for correcting the muscle tightness common to runners and orienteers.

RESOURCES

The United States Orienteering Federation (USOF) is recognized by the International Orienteering Federation (IOF) and the U.S. Olympic Committee as the official governing body for orienteering and ski-orienteering in the United States. Its purposes are to promote orienteering activities throughout the United States, to assist in establishing orienteering clubs, to establish and standardize the rules governing orienteering competition, to hold an annual national championship, to provide incentives for performance and commendable achievement in orienteering, to approve all international orienteering competitions held in the United States, and to select competitors to represent the United States in world championships.

A nonprofit corporation, its programs are supported by tax-deductible contributions. Office and committee expenses are paid for by dues and fees from its 70 member clubs and 6,000 individual members.

The USOF is staffed entirely by volunteers. The board of directors, six officers, and more than thirty committees and working groups are run by people who offer their time, energy, and expertise to make the mutual-support network function as effectively as possible.

The USOF helps its member clubs in several ways.

Competitive Expertise. Member clubs can call on various committees for advice on all aspects of orienteering. For example, the Mapping and Foreign Mappers committees can tell clubs how to make good maps at a reasonable cost. The Rules, Sanctioning, Mapping, and Course Consulting committees assist clubs holding "A" meets. The Coaching and Ranking committees aim to develop better and faster orienteers.

Program Development. A group of USOF volunteers helps clubs develop recreational and promotional programs. Clubs access these services through their local Club Development Director. Other committees work with groups, such as the Scouts, senior citizens, and military organizations. The Youth committee works with the youngest orienteers.

Administrative Efforts. The USOF provides expertise in the essential tasks needed to run a large organization, such as finance, fund-raising, insurance, computer use, magazine publication, and bylaws.

Communication. The USOF office handles membership records, public inquiries, and mailing labels for the magazine *Orienteering North America.* The USOF pages in the magazine keep members updated on official matters. The USOF serves as the communications hub for orienteers in the United States.

Other volunteer efforts are concentrated in the areas of marketing and public relations, Olympic relations, video productions, and the organizing of national competitions.

Each individual member of USOF receives a subscription to *Orienteering North America* and gets a discount of $2 each day at all "A" meets. Members may vote individually at the USOF convention and may qualify to run for officer or board positions. Members can join a USOF committee or working group, or just take advantage of their expert advice. There is a job in USOF for anyone who wants to help.

You can obtain membership and other information from member clubs or by contacting USOF, c/o Robin Shannonhouse, P.O. Box 1444, Forest Park, GA 30051, 404-363-2110.

UNITED STATES ORIENTEERING FEDERATION MEMBER CLUBS BY REGION

Northeast

Western Connecticut OC (WCOC), c/o Rick DeWitt, 390 Szost St., Fairfield, CT 06430, 203-368-9380.

New England OC (NEOC), c/o Joanne Sankus, 9 Cannon Rd., Woburn, MA 01801, 617-938-1740.

Cambridge Sports Union (CSU), c/o Larry Berman, 23 Fayette St., Cambridge, MA 02139, 617-868-7416.

Hudson Valley O' (HVO), c/o Dave Hodgdon, 106 Allentown Rd., Parsippany, NJ 07054, 201-625-0499.

Hudson Valley Orienteering (HVO), P.O. Box 61, Pleasantville, NY 10570, 201-625-0499.

Empire OC (EMPO), P.O. Box 51, Clifton Park, NY 12065, 518-877-8861.

Buffalo OC (BFLO), c/o Dave Cady, 148 Humboldt Parkway, Buffalo, NY 14214, 716-837-3737.

Rochester OC (ROC), c/o Richard Detwiler, 422 Woodland Ln., Webster, NY 14580, 716-377-5650.

Central NY O' (CNYO), c/o Barb Sleight, 6187 Smith Rd., N. Syracuse, NY 13212-2513, 315-458-6406.

Long Island OC (LIOC), c/o John Pekarik, 238 Loop Dr., Sayville, NY 11782, 516-567-5063.

Adirondack OK (AOK), c/o Brian McDonnell, 168 Lake Flower Ave., Saranac Lake, NY 12983.

U.S. Military Academy OC (USMA), c/o Dept. of Geography and Environmental Engineering, West Point, NY 10996.

Orienteering Unlimited OC (OU), c/o Ed Hicks, 3 Jan Ridge Rd., Somers, NY 10589, 914-248-5957.

Wilderness Orienteering Camps (WOC), P.O. Box 202, Mahopac, NY 10541, 914-628-7106.

Green Mountain OC (GMOC), c/o Jim Howley, 41 McIntosh Ave., S. Burlington, VT 05403, 802-862-3170.

Mid-Atlantic

Delaware Valley O' Association (DVOA), c/o Mary Frank, 14 Lake Dr., Spring City, PA 09475, 610-792-0502.

Indiana University of Pennsylvania (IUPOC), c/o Jim Wolfe, 319 Stright IUP, Indiana, PA 15705, 412-357-6104.

Susquehanna Valley Orienteering (SVO), c/o Michael Ball, 5587 Mercury Rd., Harrisburg, PA 17109.

Land of the Vikings (LOVOC), c/o Svein Sedeniussen, 270 Ehrhardt Rd., Pearl River, NY 10965, 914-735-7595.

Pocono OC (POC), P.O. Box 245, Pocono Lake, PA 18347-0245.

Warrior Ridge OC (WROC), c/o Michael Lubich, P.O. Box 191, Rice's Landing, PA 15357, 412-883-2238.

Quantico OC (QOC), 6212 Thomas Dr., Springfield, VA 22150, 703-528-4636.

Fork Union Military Academy OC (FUMA), c/o LTC Fred Tucker, Fork Union, VA 23055, 804-842-3212.

Southeast

Vulcan OC (VOC), c/o Graeme Wilson, 196 Deer Mt., Indian Springs, AL 35124.

Florida O'(FLO), c/o Frank Kuhn, 3150-334 N. Harbor City Blvd., Melbourne, FL 32935, 407-242-9480.

Georgia OC (GAOC), c/o Bill Cheatum, 1720 S. Lumpkin St., Athens, GA 30606.

Blue Star Komplex (BSK) c/o Fred Zendt, 355 Balboa Ct., Atlanta, GA 30342, 404-256-0028.

Backwoods OK (BOK), c/o Treklite, 904 Dorothea Dr., Raleigh, NC 27603, 919-828-6068.

Triad OC (TRIAD), c/o Joe Halloran, 1820 Ardsley St., Winston-Salem, NC 27103, 910-725-4203.

Carolina OK (COK), P.O. Box 220362, Charlotte, NC 28222.

Tennessee OC (TOC), c/o Meg Garrett, 1747 Murfreesboro, Hwy., Manchester, TN 37355, 615-728-2968.

Midwest

O' Louisville (OLOU), P.O. Box 7773, Louisville, KY 40257.

Southern Michigan OC (SMOC), c/o Bill Luitje, 2677 Wayside Dr., Ann Arbor, MI 48103, 313-769-7820.

North Eastern Ohio OC (NEOH), P.O. Box 5703, Cleveland, OH 44101-0703, 216-729-3255.

Orienteering Club of Cincinnati (OCIN), c/o Pat Meehan, 1306 Southern Hills Blvd., Hamilton, OH 45013-3738.

Miami Valley OC (MVOC), c/o Frederick Dudding, 2533 Far Hills Ave., Dayton, OH 45419, 513-294-2228.

Central Ohio O' (COO), c/o Michael Minium, 5412 College Corner Pike #113, Oxford, OH 45056, 513-523-9279.

Heartland

Rocky Mountain OC (RMOC), c/o Steve Willman, 710 Sunnywood Place, Woodland Park, CO 80863, 719-687-0252.

Chicago Area OC (CAOC), P.O. Box 4591, Wheaton, IL 60189, 708-397-1809.

Iowa OC (IOC), c/o Carl Thurman, 2130 Rainbow Dr., Waterloo, IA 50701, 319-273-2276 (D), 319-232-1405 (N).

Orienteer Kansas (OK), c/o Gene Wee, 2223 Westchester Rd., Lawrence, KS 66049.

Possum Trot OC (PTOC), c/o Alan Cowles, 11512 W. 101st Terr., Overland Park, KS 66214.

Minnesota OC (MNOC), P.O. Box 580030, Minneapolis, MN 55458, 612-226-2118.

St. Louis OC (SLOC), c/o Al Smith, 74 Decorah Dr., St. Louis, MO 63146, 314-872-3165.

North Dakota O'Alliance (NDOA), c/o Michelle Keller, P.O. Box 265, Bisbee, ND 58317, 701-656-3435.

Badger OC (BGR), c/o Catherine Ann Yekenevicz, 868 Weslyn Ct., #2, West Bend, WI 53095, 414-335-3304.

Southwest

ARK-LA-TEX-O-SOCIETY (ALTOS), P.O. Box 8792, Bossier City, LA 71113-8792, 318-949-3601.

Sooner OC (SOON), c/o Paul Akin, 4524 S. Irvington, Tulsa, OK 74235, 918-663-9266.

Houston OC (HOC), c/o Carolyn Ortegon, P.O. Box 18251, Houston, TX 77023, 713-484-1391.

North Texas O Assn. (NTOA), P.O. Box 832464, Richardson, TX 75083-2464, 214-385-8952.

Hill Country OC (HCOC), c/o Steve Nelson, 45 Eskew Lane, Cedar Creek, TX 78612.

Aggie Pathfinders (AGGIE), P.O. Box 8592, College Station, TX 77844, 409-847-4530.

Pacific

Tucson OC (TSN), P. O. Box 13012, Tucson, AZ 85732, 602-628-8985.

Phoenix OC (PHXO), c/o Fred Padgett, 2031 N. 16th St., Phoenix, AZ 85006, 602-956-7522.

Bay Area OC (BAOC), c/o Gary Kraght, 518 Park Way, Mill Valley, CA 94941, 408-255-8018.

Los Angeles OC (LAOC), c/o Clare Durand, 5341 Wilkinson Ave. #3, N. Hollywood, CA 91607, 818-769-0906.

San Diego Orienteering (SDO), c/o Bill Gookin, P.O. Box 26722, San Diego, CA 92196, 619-578-9456.

Gold Country Orienteers (GCO), c/o Dwight Freund, 2948 Leta Lane, Sacramento, CA 95821, 916-481-2850.

Utah Governor's Council on Health and Physical Fitness, c/o Darlene Uzelac, P.O. Box 16660, Salt Lake City, UT 84116.

Northwest

Arctic OC (ARCT), c/o Daniel Ellsworth, 6436 Carlos Ct., Anchorage, AK 99504.

Columbia River OC (CROC), c/o Matthew Boser, 1700 NE 162nd Ave. #E2, Portland, OR 97230, 503-251-4779.

Jefferson State OC (JSOC), c/o Allyson Kelley, P.O. Box 1371, Medford, OR 97501, 503-535-3104.

Cascade OC (COC), P.O. Box 31375, Seattle, WA 98103, 206-783-3866.

Chuckanut Orienteers (CHUKO), c/o Ken & Joanne Klepsch, 4313 Tyler Way, Anacortes, WA 98221.

Eastern Washington OC (EWOC), P.O. Box 944, Spokane, WA 99210, 509-838-7078.

Ellensburg OC (EOC), c/o Willard Sperry, 1006 N. Water St., Ellensburg, WA 98926.

Husky OC (HUSKY), c/o Eric Bone, HUB 207 FK-30, Box 118, University of Washington, Seattle, WA 98195, 206-634-2279.

Nisqually O' (NISQ), c/o Carl Moore, 1453 N. Winnifred, Tacoma, WA 98406, 206-756-5739.

Sacajawea Orienteers (SACO), c/o Elis Eberlein, 520 Meadows Dr. S., Richland, WA 99352, 509-627-0378.

Sammamish OC (SAMM), P.O. Box 3682, Bellevue, WA 98009, 206-822-6254.

If there is no club in your area and you'd like to form one, contact the **United States Orienteering Federation** at P.O. Box 1444, Forest Park, GA 30051, 404-363-2110.